Oriental Rugs

TODAY

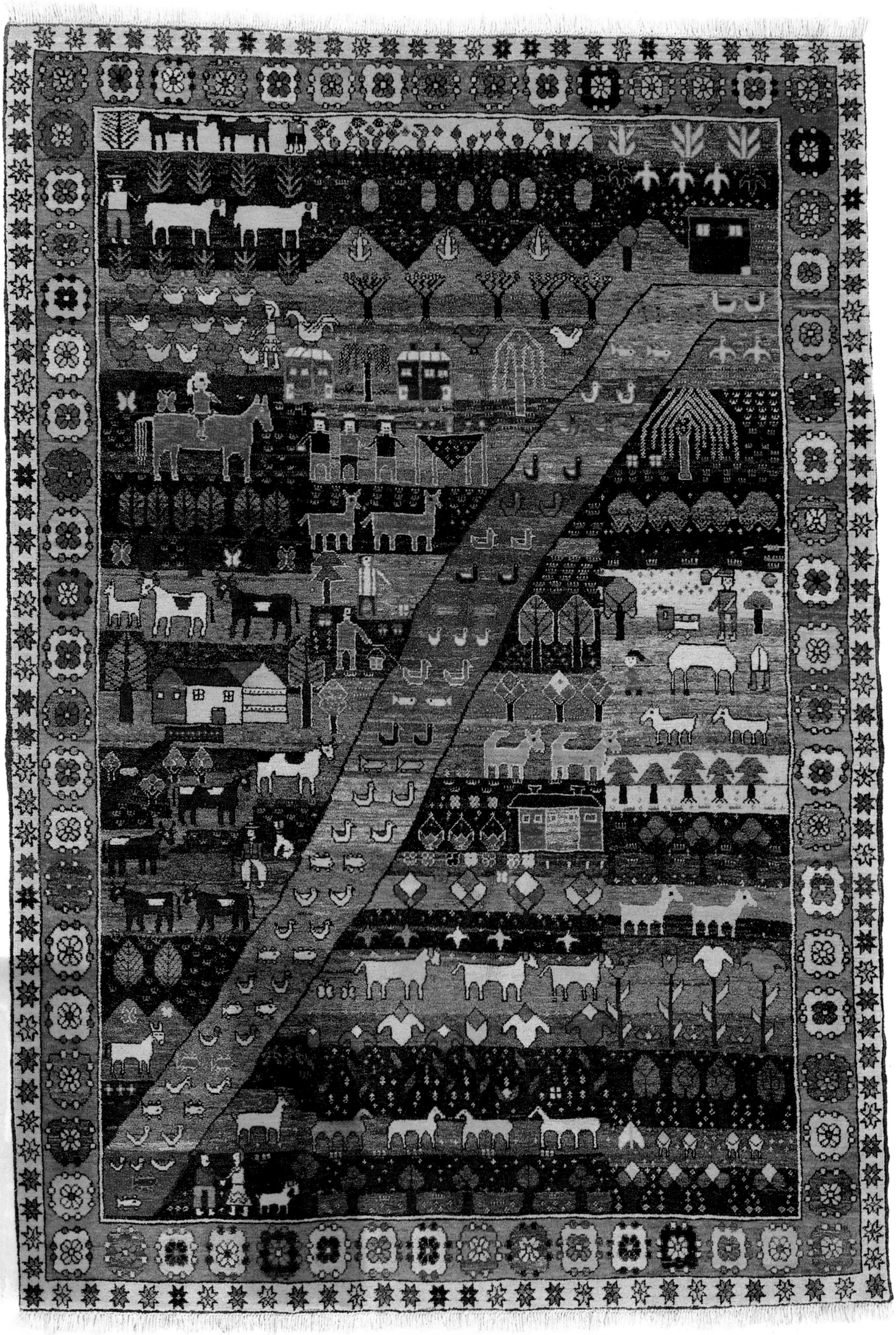

Oriental Rugs
TODAY

A Guide to the Best in New
Carpets from the East

Emmett Eiland

Berkeley Hills Books
Berkeley, California

Published by
Berkeley Hills Books, PO Box 9877, Berkeley CA 94709
www.berkeleyhills.com

Distributed by Publishers Group West

Library of Congress Cataloging-in-Publication Data

Eiland, Emmett, 1941–
        Oriental rugs today : a guide to the best in new carpets from the
East / Emmett Eiland.
            p.   cm.
        ISBN 1-893163-03-2 (alk. paper)
        1. Rugs, Oriental––History––20th century.   I. Title.
        NK2808.E43   1999
        746. 7' 5' 095––dc21   99-39180

Designed by Design Site, Berkeley CA

Color separations and printing by Snow Lion Graphics, Berkeley/Hong Kong

1 3 5 7 9 10 8 6 4 2

To

A. Cecil Edwards

who, after a lifetime in the Oriental rug business, surveyed the new rugs of his day and left a record of them in a book that still may be the best ever written about Oriental rugs: The Persian Carpet *(London 1953). Like generations of other writers on the subject, I have been inspired by his obvious love of rugs, by his care in describing them, and by the humanism that quietly pervades his writing.*

Acknowledgments

During the past months, I have learned why husbands who write books thank their wives first and foremost. Mine, Natasha Eiland, has encouraged me at dark moments and looked after our quality of life while I worked on the book, all without complaint. Natasha, thank you. I have many others to thank, too. I am very grateful to Paul Ramsey, George Postrozny, Nick Baloff, Jack Simantob, Stephanie Odegard, Al Gertmenian, Paul Gertmenian, Haynes Robinson, James Tufenkian, Chris Walter, Steve Laska, George Jevremovic, Teddy Sumner, David Samad, Malcolm Samad, Tom Franklin, Berislav Kuntic, Paul McSweeny, Ahmad Ahmadi, Hamayoon Mosenpour, Mason Purcell, Mike Marci, Iraj Noorollah, Wenjun Cheng, Lee Haroonian, Keith DeMare, Anjum Butt, Yeran Megerian, Jerry Aziz, Kesang Tashi, Bill McDonnell, and Izi Mizrahi. Thank you Elizabeth Delphy, Sharon Schenck, Barry O'Connell, Jim Opie, Rich Asadorian, Sam Presnell, and Sarkis Tatosian. Thank you David Walker, David Holbrook Young, and Don Tuttle. Thanks to Joe Bezdjian, Lew Wheeler, Sylvette Orlianges, Carolyn Garnier, Jesse Eiland, Paul Ehrhorn, and Allen Gains. And finally my deep appreciation to my publisher, Berkeley Hills Books, and to Robert Dobbin, whose particular project this was. Rob, who had not before published an Oriental rug book, began our discussions about the project by asking whether eight color plates would be adequate and eventually told me, 'Do what you want about color plates!' Thank you for your generosity, vision, encouragement and, in the best Berkeley tradition, good vibes.

DISCLAIMER ABOUT PRICES

From time to time in these pages I have given approximate retail prices for particular rugs. Please do not treat these prices as carved in stone—they aren't. Every retailer is free to choose what he or she believes is right, and prices will vary. This book is not intended as a price guide. Buyers should do their own shopping for price and not base their decision on my figures alone.

A SUGGESTION

You will learn more and enjoy this book more if you have a good magnifying glass on hand to view the plates. I recommend the type that rests on the page at just the right height so that the photo is in focus. Many of the plates are devoted to demonstrating differences between hand-spun and machine-spun wool, natural and synthetic dyes, and so on. A good glass can do wonders. It can even suggest something about the texture of rugs, an important facet of carpets otherwise not accessible on the pages of a book. Viewing photos of rugs with a magnifying glass is like taking a walk through a garden, as opposed to merely viewing it from the veranda: it's more engaging and more fun.

CONTENTS

PART ONE

BACKGROUND TO THE RUGS

"I fear that I will disappoint readers who have been led to believe that designs in Oriental rugs spring from the collective unconscious of primitive weavers, that every Oriental rug tells a symbolic story, and so on. I've always believed that Oriental rugs are miraculous enough without resorting to hype."

The best *new* Oriental carpets, woven now at the dawning of the twenty-first century, are more beautiful and of better quality than any woven in the past seventy years. Less expensive than antique rugs and in perfect condition, they represent an opportunity for buyers. But shoppers for new carpets need to know much more about them than they did just a few years ago when choices were fewer. Existing books on Oriental carpets, preoccupied with antique rugs, are not of much use. *Oriental Rugs Today* surveys the new rugs and carpets on the market, sorts the wheat from the chaff, and discusses the issues you need to know in order to make good choices among modern Oriental rugs.

Why are Oriental rugs suddenly so good? Some weavers have rediscovered techniques and materials and designs that seemed to be lost forever, and are weaving rugs almost exactly as they were made 2500 years ago. A few dyers are once again creating colors from natural plant dyes, and

A Yatak from Woven Legends. Its Turkish weaver evidently has been given great latitude to improvise. One surmises that she is still learning.

now a sizeable number of spinners spin by hand the wool from which rugs are made. Missing from rugs for decades, the very best designs of the past two hundred years have been restored to the weavers' repertoire. Other weavers experiment with contemporary designs, adding a whole new dimension to Oriental rugs. Modern technology in communications, travel, and information are doing their part to transform the market. To give an example: A made-to-order 9 by 12-foot carpet can now be woven in Nepal and delivered to your door in a mere three months, still knotted by hand in the traditional manner.

Certain aspects of Oriental rugs have changed so fast and dramatically that people who walk into a rug store for the first time in ten years are captivated, but puzzled. Almost nothing that was true of the market a decade ago applies today. Some people are only vaguely aware that America boycotts Persian (Iranian) rugs, and are surprised to learn that Persian rugs are hardly a factor at all now in America's new rug market. The last they knew, Chinese rugs still looked like Chinese rugs (!), and new rugs were invariably made with synthetic dyes. They assume that to buy a rug with soft colors and natural dyes they will have to purchase an antique. It takes some time for them to adjust to the notion that today they can spend far less money and buy a *new* rug with natural dyes. They are especially surprised that Indian rugs are no longer the inferior products they once were, but instead are among the best and most interesting on the market. And it comes as a shock to learn that Pakistan, now populated by hundreds of thousands of rug-weaving refugees from Afghanistan, produces among the most desirable rugs in the world. Above all, the new rugs that people see on showroom walls look startlingly good to them.

During the past 100 years, Oriental rug weaving has come full circle: a fertile period from 1880 to 1920, a period of decline that lasted about sixty-five years, succeeded now by a new golden age that began around 1985. Is 'renaissance' the right word for what Oriental rugs are going through? 'A renewal of life, vigor, interest, etc.; rebirth, revival'— according to my dictionary. Yes, but it is more: The original Renaissance, in Italy, also involved a rediscovery of older artistic ideas and antique composition (like the traditional designs again revered in rugs), a return to nature and

A new rug that easily could be mistaken for an antique. Note the repair along the selvage. It was made in Pakistan by Art Resources of Los Angeles after an old 'Camel' Hamadan from Iran. It was not the rugmaker's intention to deceive, simply to make a new rug that looks as good as an old one. Approximately 4' by 6'. Natural dye, handspun wool pile. (David Holbrook Young.)

naturalism (like the rediscovery of natural dyes and handspun wool), and a new sense of freedom—like the way some rugmakers now feel at liberty to innovate their own designs. 'Renaissance' is the *perfect* word to describe what we are going through.

Not everyone agrees with me, though, that we have entered a period of exceptional rug weaving. A respected colleague argues that only a small percentage of the rugs in the market now are extraordinary, possibly less than 5 percent. In the Midwest, he says, dealers are selling essentially the same rugs they sold fifteen years ago. The rugmakers I admire, he says, are hardly players at all in the rug world, compared to the giant New York firms that every month produce thousands of square meters of more plebeian carpets. My thesis that we are living in a golden age of Oriental rugs, he says, is 'controversial'. (I suspect he means ' wrong'.)

He is quite right that the extraordinary is outnumbered by the ordinary, and I am sure that is how it has always been in periods of great rug weaving—or painting, or architecture, or sculpture. Rug dealers in some communities may continue to show the rugs they showed fifteen years ago. But that hardly means that a renaissance has not taken place. What it means to me is that another rug dealer in the same community is liable to get a jump on them by showing customers the really wonderful rugs that simply weren't around until recently. Although great new Oriental rugs may number only 5 percent of all rugs woven today, that is 100 percent more great rugs than were woven twenty years ago. What matters is that 100 percent of the rugs and carpets in *your* home may be among the 5 percent that are great.

You may find some general information useful. Shoppers for new carpets now have the opportunity to choose between vegetal and synthetic dyes, and between hand-spun and machine-spun wool. You can choose between new rugs that look new, and new rugs that look old. These are more than academic matters: the cost of a rug will be determined by such choices and so will its quality. Buyers are also faced with confusing labels. For instance, the same rug in different stores might be labeled 'Mahal', 'Sultanabad', 'Pakistani', 'Turkmen', 'Aryana', and 'Yayla', or some combination of these, like

'Turkmen Mahal'—each with justification. (Recently my company was invoiced for a new rug as follows: 'Ireland Mongol Aztec Green.' The rug was woven in China.) How can you make sense of something like that?

Most books on Oriental rugs don't help. Very few of the ones in print even touch on the subject of new rugs, and almost none written in the last twenty years discuss new rugs in depth. They are geared to collectors of antique carpets, and do an admirable job of describing rugs of the nineteenth and early twentieth centuries. Their authors explain that a weaver's designs are inherited from her mother, who in turn inherited designs from her mother, and so on. But today the world is different. Take the improbable but actual example of Turkmen weavers from Afghanistan now living as refugees in Pakistan: while some weave their traditional Turkmen designs, most make rugs for Americans and Europeans from nine-teenth-century north Persian or Caucasian designs. Few rug books help you understand those rugs or others actually in rug stores today. (One hint: hyphenated labels purport to give the rug's origin, followed by the source of its design. Thus an Indo-Bijar is from India, in a traditional Bijar pattern from Persia.)

I wrote this book to help guide you through the brave new world of Oriental rugs. It is designed to give you information you need to make your own decisions—and to have fun while doing it. I have not intended this to be a dry, academic book, though I have worked hard to keep it factual, and have resisted the temptation to romanticize Oriental rugs. I've often taken the reader to their back-stage world, where things are often less glamorous than from where the audience sits. I fear that I will disappoint readers who have been led to believe that designs in Oriental rugs spring from the collective unconscious of primitive weavers, that every Oriental rug tells a symbolic story, and so on. I've always believed that Oriental rugs are miraculous enough without resorting to hype.

I will admit to another purpose: I would like to shake up those who believe that good rugs ceased to be made in 1250, or 1700, or 1850, or 1920. (I myself thought along those lines for around twenty years.) Some of the rugs in these color plates should be evidence enough that this prejudice is wrong. There are many new rugs out there today that are really, really good!

And I have had one last goal on my agenda. The carpets in this book are *our* carpets; they are the rugs of the twenty-first century. They will become semi-antiques during the next century, and a few will live on even as the next century wanes. A very few, by some chance, may even survive for 1000 years. It pleases me to think that some day long from now a scholar, seeking to solve the mystery of a rug found locked away, wondering when it was made and by whom, may read this book and find in it a photograph and information recorded when the rug was new, and say, 'Aha! That's it!'

There are many carpets in the market today that are simply wonderful. There is no question in my mind that this Azeri will one day be acknowledged to have been woven during a golden age of rugmaking.

Chapter 1

The Rug Renaissance

Tomorrow's antique. A new carpet from Megerian Brothers of New York.
How will rug scholars know 100 years from now that it was made in Egypt?

Americans and Europeans of a certain stripe have been in love with Oriental rugs for over a century. But we have preferred old rugs to new. Nearly all collectors and many home decorators have perceived a beauty in the soft colors and polished wool of rugs that have been walked upon for decades, and they have found new Oriental rugs too bright. Before the twentieth century, Americans imported old rugs almost exclusively, and began to buy new rugs only when the supply of good old pieces in the Middle East was exhausted. (For more on this, see Edwards, *The Persian Carpet* , pages 55–56.) No doubt our preference for old rugs was merely a cultural prejudice. The people who made them rather liked the cheerful colors of new rugs. But as the twentieth century wore on, Americans seemed to have more grounds for their prejudice, because over the early and middle decades of the century weavers gradually abandoned the use of their traditional, vegetal dyestuffs and substituted synthetic dyes of poor quality. Certain early synthetics quickly faded into nothingness (from purple to almost no color, for instance), others bled when exposed to water, and some colors never lost an irritating, overly bright quality...and never will. By shortly after World War II, for all practical purposes, natural dyes in Oriental rugs were a thing of the past. The only way one could own a rug with natural dyes was to buy an old one. Of course, as the quality of new rugs declined, the cost of old rugs began to rise.

As the twentieth century progressed, rugs showed a decline in quality far beyond their loss of natural dyes. In the disruption of two world wars, many rug weavers were unable to transmit traditional designs and techniques to their daughters, and designs associated with certain villages and tribes disappeared. In fact, the rug production of whole

Heriz from about 1935. Earlier Herizes were relatively simple and open. By 1935 they had become busy and cluttered—like this example.

countries was lost to the West because of political conditions. For many years, for instance, the Cold War between the Soviet Union and the West deprived us of Caucasian and many Turkmen rugs, and hostilities between the West and China made new Chinese rugs unavailable. By the 1950s, there simply were fewer new rugs to choose from than there had been in the past, and many of the ones available to us showed unmistakable deterioration. Oddly, as weaving skills were lost, rug designs often seemed to become more elaborate, resulting in new rugs that were 'busy'—crowded and confusing.

Materials in rugs suffered too, as the price of good wool rose after World War II and weavers substituted cheaper wool shorn from dead sheep. The one bit of good news was that synthetic dyes had improved enormously. By the 1950s, modern chrome dyes had nearly eliminated radical fading and bleeding, and the 'edginess' of some early synthetic colors was no longer in evidence. But with this one exception, the quality of carpets overall fell from about 1925 into the 1980s. As new rugs became less desirable, antiques became more and more expensive. Many Americans simply dropped out of the Oriental rug market and discovered the charms of wall-to-wall carpeting.

When my brother Murray Eiland and I opened the doors of our Oriental rug store in 1969 (Murray was then just beginning to work on a book that subsequently became a very successful guide to antique Oriental rugs), our inventory consisted of old rugs almost entirely. It is true that our first love was antiques, but we wanted to carry a stock of new rugs too. There just weren't many that looked good to us. Qums, Isfahans, and Nains from Iran were finely knotted, but stiff-looking and expensive. Heriz carpets were dominated by a very bright synthetic red. Afghans

A new 'Heriz' made in Pakistan by Turkmen refugees. Its designer has returned to the simplicity and the spare feeling of very old Serapis. It has been woven from handspun, natural-dyed wool. Made by Yayla Tribal Rugs, this carpet is about 8' by 12' and is called Aryana. (Don Tuttle.)

(as Ersari Turkmen rugs were then called) were two-color rugs of red and a blue so dark it appeared black. A little later, Mishkins, Ardabiles, and Tabatabai Tabriz rugs appeared in the market. They were affordable and attractive, and we bought a few. But, by and large, new rugs and carpets were pretty dismal things.

As I say, there were exceptions. In retrospect, I believe many of the Indian and Pakistani rugs we bought and sold then, and the Romanian rugs we traded a few years later, were better than we realized. I have watched as these rugs have come back to the shop for washing, and they have softened and picked up a nice luster with use. On trips to Turkey and Afghanistan we found good tribal rugs, piece by piece. And we could always find things to buy in Iran with its vast markets; Iran was still a bright spot. But political clouds were gathering in Iran and we knew it.

In the fall of 1979, my wife, Natasha, and I were bound for Iran (brother Murray and I were no longer partners) for what we feared might be our last buying trip before things really soured with Iran. Just before we left, we wrote a radio ad suggesting that this might be a good time to buy Persian rugs: prices were still good, but everything could change fast. They did. Just as the ad ran, the Persians took sixty-six Americans hostage, and we arrived at the airport in Tehran unaware of what had happened. Fortunately we were never allowed off the airplane, but we had to sit in it for many hours while Persian officials held our passports.

Eventually our Pan Am flight was allowed to leave, loaded with Americans fleeing Iran. In the meantime, the radio station back home on which the ad was playing received seventy angry complaints from people who thought we were trying to capitalize on the hostage crisis. From then until 1987, it was possible for Americans to import rugs from Iran, but (to borrow a contemporary expression) Persian rugs were not 'politically correct'. After 1987, all trade with Iran, which had been by far the largest source of Oriental rugs to the United States, ceased. The sad state of the new rug market, at least in America, was worse than ever.

By the 1980s, dealers with high standards were desperate for merchandise. Each week, sales reps from importers based in New York canvassed my

This is a good example of the degraded state to which Turkmen rugs (often simply called Afghans in those days) had been reduced by about 1970. It has only two colors, both are from synthetic dyes. It is an Ersari from Afghanistan, about 3' by 4'.

store and showed samples of their latest goods, which looked exactly like their previous stock and like the rugs every other New York firm was importing. Most were made in India. On the rare occasions that someone would come up with a new design, all the other wholesalers copied it in a matter of months. We bought the best of these rugs but wished for better, and we continued selling antique rugs and carpets as they became scarcer all the time. It looked as if soon we wouldn't have anything to sell at all.

In contrast to the previous rug, this new Turkmen is full of charm and natural dyes. Its five colors are just like the colors in Turkmen rugs from 150 years ago. It was made in 1998 by Turkmen weavers in northwestern Pakistan and is one of the Ersari Turkmen Cultural Survival rugs. Approximately 3' by 4'. (David Holbrook Young.)

Suddenly, or so it seems, the 'dark ages' of Oriental rugs of the past sixty years has given way to a renaissance, expressed beautifully in this Egyptian carpet woven by Megerian Brothers of New York.

These days I survey new rugs and carpets as they come available, and I find myself unable to suppress that old competitive, acquisitive feeling familiar from earlier years when I was on the trail of good antique rugs. Natasha and I come across new carpets with designs we have seen only in museums. We find rugs that are full of character, rugs with vegetal dyes and handspun wool, gorgeous rugs— and a lot of them, more than we can afford to buy. At some time, unnoticed at first, the world of Oriental rugs entered a renaissance. How did it happen? When did it happen?

I have gone over our inventory records for the past thirty years to learn when the first exceptional rugs began to appear. I have thought back on the young adventurers I knew who went off to Turkey and Nepal and Iran in the '70s and the trips I made there myself in those years. I came back home to run a rug store without it occurring to me to make rugs or have them made. But others stayed, learned the languages, and helped create a renaissance in rugs ten years later.

I believe the story of the renaissance begins during the 1960s when deep social changes took place in America that affected even the Oriental rug industry. One of the trends in the '60s was a preference for lifestyles and objects that seemed natural and pure, simple and primitive. That spirit was healthy for the Oriental rug industry, for, under its influence, Americans finally began to lose their taste for wall-to-wall carpeting, which had been the industry's scourge during the '40s and '50s. By the end of the '60s, many Americans found that they preferred Oriental to machine-made rugs, and they especially liked the ones weavers made out beside their tents. If previous generations of rug lovers had been enthralled by the exquisite detail and perfection of rugs from Persian cities, in the '60s and into the '70s and '80s many were drawn by the whimsical irregularities of tribal and village textiles. After appealing to relatively few people for about thirty years, Oriental rugs were back, spearheaded by a fascination with tribal and village rugs, whose popularity grew even stronger in the '70s, '80s, and '90s.

The powerful appeal of old tribal and village rugs like this antique Caucasian piece drove the market from about 1970 to roughly 1985. New rugs of that era were simply not as attractive. The 'renaissance' began, I believe, about 1985, when a few rugmakers managed to capture the character of old tribal and village rugs from Turkey, the Caucasus, and northern Iran.

The current that engendered this change in fashion was powerful enough to influence lives. Some young college-educated Americans, most of whose parents had hardly been aware of Oriental rugs, chose to make careers of them. As the '70s progressed, a few adventurous young rug dealers struck out for exotic countries on a quest for Oriental rugs and a life of adventure.

During those years as a rug dealer, I was asked to speak on the subject by nearly every civic and art-oriented group in town. A doctor's wife volunteered to repair rugs in my shop simply for the sake of spending time with them. Many bright young women pursued careers in my shop restoring rugs—and there was enough interest in rugs among the townspeople to keep all these repairers employed. Interest in Oriental rugs went far beyond decorating with them.

There was one problem, though. Only antique rugs were attractive enough to satisfy the appetite of collectors, home decorators, and dealers in tribal and village rugs—and antiques were scarce and expensive. *New* pieces—and there were a few coming into the market—had the sour colors associated with synthetic dyes: edgy orange, for instance, and a very bright pink. If Americans were nearly united in their love for tribal and village rugs, they were equally decided about disliking edgy orange and bright pink. It was widely believed that the art of natural dyeing had been lost forever, and I don't believe it crossed many minds that new rugs had the potential to offer a satisfying and relatively inexpensive alternative to antique tribal pieces.

Then along came a German schoolteacher who changed the modern history of Oriental rugs. Harald Böhmer, a chemistry professor, went to Turkey to teach in 1960, and while there he became interested in the dyes he found in Turkish rugs and kilims. By the time his tenure expired in 1967, he was in love with rugs and with Turkey, and in 1974 signed a contract for another seven years of teaching there. By then he was methodically analyzing the dyes in Turkish carpets, enabled by a new technique called thin layer chromatography. He was especially interested in natural dyes, and he endeavored to reconstruct exactly how they had been constituted and prepared. Faced with having to return to Germany when his contract ended, he

A Yürük girl working on a kilim. She is using a heavy comb-like beater to compact the wefts. Turkish village, 1985. (Chris Walter.)

conceived the idea of reviving the use of natural dyes among Turkish village rug weavers. He managed to get his idea funded and, by 1981, had taught weavers in villages around Ayvacik in western Turkey to produce rugs in natural dyes. The project, called DOBAG (an acronym for *Dogal Boya Arastirma ve Gelistirme Projesi*—Turkish for Natural Dye Research and Development Project), was an almost instant success. Within a few years, not only were hundreds of weavers involved in selling their natural-dyed rugs through the DOBAG cooperative, but weavers in nearby villages were learning to use natural dyes and were selling rugs in the open market. At just that time, in the early days of DOBAG, a number of young Americans were traveling in Turkey and trading in rugs there. Two who staged their trips from Berkeley were Gary Muse, who later succeeded in putting together one of the world's great collections of antique Turkish kilims, and Saul Barodosky, now of the Sunbow Trading Company in Charlottesville, Virginia. They remained focused on old rugs, but other Americans involved with old rugs, like Chris Walter and George Jevremovic, found themselves interested in the new, natural-dyed ones from DOBAG and surrounding villages. Within a few years, both Mr. Walter and Mr. Jevremovic had established productions of vegetal-dyed rugs in tribal and village designs that, along with the DOBAG project itself, profoundly changed the Oriental rug industry. (George Jevremovic and Chris Walter's stories, along with those of other movers and shakers of the rug renaissance, are told in greater detail in Part Two.) In Turkey, we can clearly trace the progression of the natural dye movement: Harald Böhmer helped establish DOBAG in 1980; DOBAG weavers and weavers from surrounding villages began to produce significant quantities of vegetal-dyed rugs; George Jevremovic was impressed and began his own production in Turkey in about 1984; from that

A Turkish village rug from the DOBAG collective. With their traditional village designs, natural dyes, and handspun wool, rugs like this one were nothing short of revolutionary in the early '80s.

point onward, nearly everyone making rugs in Turkey and elsewhere was influenced by DOBAG and especially by Mr. Jevremovic's Azeri rugs. One of the important contributions George Jevremovic made to the renaissance was producing rugs with a tribal character in carpet—that is, large—sizes. Before that, room-sized carpets in tribal designs were practically nonexistent.

The rug renaissance was under way and being felt—if not yet identified as such—in America by 1985. One of the most important factors that helped it grow was George Jevremovic's talent for promotion. He had a perfect understanding of how attractive to the rug-buying public the concept was of rediscovering the seemingly lost art of natural dyeing. He promoted it in poetic language, focusing on the weavers' art. Mr. Jevremovic mounted exhibitions of his carpets—possibly the first exhibitions of new Oriental rugs—and he wrote books about them. He set a precedent by advertising his new rugs in *Hali*, the leading

An early Azeri from Woven Legends. The nascent renaissance in Oriental rugs moved a step forward in the middle and late 1980s when Woven Legends released carpets like this. Its outrageous asymmetry, its huge borders and giant design elements, its playfulness, its lavish natural dyes—all were without precedent. And this is not a little tribal throw rug; it is a 7 by 9-foot carpet.

journal devoted (originally) to antique rugs. To a large extent, he created the market for new, natural-dyed tribal rugs. The DOBAG people also did a marvelous job of promoting them, but they limited the effectiveness of their efforts by restricting the sale of them to specialty stores. I count George Jevremovic's wise promotion of his product as one of the most important factors behind the popularity of new rugs after 1985. Once natural dyeing was established, Phase One of the renaissance was complete.

In the meantime, another important change in fashion was beginning to take shape in the Oriental rug industry, a trend toward what became known as decorative carpets. For whatever reason, the public was beginning to favor carpets that were formal looking and light in color— almost the opposite of village and tribal rugs. In a kind of cosmic perversity, the trend began just when the rug industry was finally able to meet the need for relatively inexpensive tribal rugs and carpets: that is, around 1985. If Phase One of the rug renaissance was fueled by public demand for rugs with a genuine tribal or village look, Phase Two would be propelled by the market's demand for decorative carpets.

While some Western youths were exploring Turkey in the '70s and '80s, others were setting off for adventures with Tibetan Buddhism and the rug industry in Nepal. In Katmandu they met thousands of Tibetans who had fled Chinese-occupied Tibet beginning in the 1950s. The Tibetans brought a knowledge of rugmaking with them, along with their traditional designs, and they forged a Nepalese carpet industry where none had existed before. That industry, whose principal customers were the Germans, kept many refugees alive, and the rugs they made charmed many a Western youth living in Nepal.

Some of the Americans who came to Nepal in the late '70s and early '80s were interested in natural dyes, but the rugs they encountered were made with synthetics. The secrets of natural dyeing had survived among only a handful of Tibetan refugees. Among them were brothers Tsetan and Dorje, and an associate named Namgyl who ran a store in Katmandu called Vegetable Dyed Carpets. One young American, called Tombo (Thomas Guta, discussed at greater length in Chapter Five), was making rugs with natural dyes and selling them to tourists. Apparently he had been in Nepal since the mid '70s or earlier, and had learned natural dyeing from one of the Tibetan refugees, most likely either Tsetan or Namgyl. Tombo may have been the first American to make Oriental rugs with natural dyes. Other Americans who were in Nepal during that period began to have rugs made for export, and, influenced by Tombo and his Tibetan mentors, the first rugs they produced were in vegetal dyes. So, on a modest scale, a natural dye rug industry was established in Katmandu by about 1980, at almost exactly the same time that Harald Böhmer established what was known as the DOBAG project in Turkey. But by 1987, natural dyeing was nearly dead in Nepal. Germans began buying Tibetan rugs very heavily at around that time. They wanted large quantities at low prices, and the Tibetan industry geared up to provide it. Natural dyes, being expensive, fell into disuse, and for the next several years were all but forgotten again.

Nevertheless, Western rugmakers in Nepal, in partnership with their Tibetan producers, made important contributions to what became the rug renaissance. It seems that a number of European and American rugmakers realized at about the same time (around 1985) that rugs could be made in Nepal in all kinds of designs and colors, and not just in traditional Tibetan designs. James Tufenkian, Stephanie Odegard, Teddy Sumner, Steve Laska—these pioneers took aim at the new demand for decorative carpets, designing rugs with soft, light, low-contrast colors and simple, though formal, patterns. Together they created a wonderful diversity of rugs that were different from anything that had been in the market before, and launched the first major decorative rug productions.

The rugs that were made by Westerners in Turkey and Nepal—often in partnership with native rug producers— were commercially successful, and stimulated legions of others to launch their own productions and to experiment with natural dyes and new designs. The state of decline in which rugs had been locked for the previous sixty years was halted. From about 1985 on, new rugs simply got better and better and are improving still.

This is one of a new generation of Tibetan rugs from about 1987. I believe that American and European rugmakers in Nepal were among the first to sense the need for what we now call decorative carpets—carpets, that is, with light, soft, low-contrast colors, and an inviting texture. Decorative carpets now drive the market in the way that tribal rugs did until about 1985. This Tibetan rug was made by Endless Knot Trading Company in Petaluma, California and is about 6' by 9'.

Besides the movement of Tibetans into Nepal after China's invasion of Tibet, several other international political events helped the rug renaissance along—although, for many of the people caught up in them, the consequences were disastrous. The first was the Soviet invasion of Afghanistan in 1979, and Afghanistan's subsequent civil war. These events forced the exodus of more than a million people from Afghanistan to Pakistan where they have since lived as refugees in giant camps near the Afghan border. Like the Tibetan refugees in Nepal, one of the very few ways they have had of generating money is by weaving. But the creation of their traditional designs has been disrupted. One can imagine that, thrown together in the camps rather than dispersed among small villages as they had been in Afghanistan, they became aware of the sameness of their rugs and the difficulty of selling rugs that look just like everyone else's. So thousands of skilled weavers became available to weave rugs under contract, willing to create whatever they were paid to. Anyone with the means can have rugs made in the refugee camps in designs of their choice.

Chris Walter, from Cambridge, Massachusetts, in partnership with a Turkmen named Jora Agha, established the first production of rugs in Pakistan with natural dyes in 1987. That production and Chris Walter's subsequent vegetal dye projects were enormously successful, and paved the way for natural dye productions by scores, possibly hundreds, of other Westerners who are turning out some of the best rugs made in the past seventy years, both tribal and decorative. It is unlikely that any of this would have happened had Afghan weavers not been forced from home. I count the establishment of the Afghan refugee camps in Pakistan as among the most important conditions contributing to the renaissance—as unfortunate as it was in other respects. But I must add that it was not conditions but people of vision like Chris Walter and Jora Agha who made the renaissance happen.

Another international political event affecting rug production was the Islamic Revolution in Iran in 1979. It led to a complete U.S. boycott of Iranian carpets by 1987. That was a very frightening development for most American rug dealers. (Europeans have continued to buy carpets from Iran.) It meant the loss of our largest source of Oriental rugs. But a decade later, it looks to me like a blessing in disguise—for two reasons. First, it stimulated other countries such as India to improve the quality of their rugs. But even more important, losing Iran forced us to take our business to countries that were more responsive to Western needs than Iran had ever been. Persian weavers have always been uncompromising— stubborn, even. Simply getting Persian weavers to produce carpets in American sizes, for instance, has been impossible. (We need 8 by 10-foot rugs for our dining rooms, for example, but few weavers will comply. They make rugs in meter sizes, and the closest most Persian carpets come to 8 by 10 is about 6' 10" by 10' 8".) Eager for our business, Indian rugmakers will make rugs in any size. They cooperate in all respects, weaving designs submitted by Westerners, using the colors we request and going so far as to re-learn the art of dyeing rugs with vegetal substances and the craft of spinning wool by hand. Similarly, because of our boycott of Iranian carpets, Americans became more reliant on China. During the past eight to ten years, Westerners have had rugs woven there with vegetal dyes and handspun wool that are, in my opinion, better than anything that has come out of Iran in the last sixty years. China, too, is much more willing to accommodate Western needs than Iran ever was. In fact, all the countries Americans turned to when we lost Iran as a source of rugs have been willing and able to work with American rugmakers and importers. The result is that, while we have lost Iran's marvelous rugs, we have gained far more control over the rugs produced for our market. This has allowed Americans like Teddy Sumner, George Jevremovic, and others to make superb carpets in China and India that likely would never have been made had trade with Iran not been interrupted.

One last factor has motivated the renaissance, and that is technology. It is perhaps surprising that a low-tech industry like Oriental rugs could benefit from twentieth-century technology. But that is the case. First of all, the information available to Western rugmakers is unimaginably richer than that available to weavers in, say, northern Afghanistan—or, for that matter, to Westerners thirty years ago. Improvements in the technology of making color separations, by which color plates are prepared for publication, have lowered their prices so greatly that today it is not uncommon to find rug books with 100 color

A Little River carpet from Black Mountain Looms. Black Mountain Looms, in its formative stage, flew a spinner from Boulder, Colorado to teach Chinese weavers to spin wool by hand.

plates or more. Today Western rugmakers have at their disposal thousands of reproductions of the best Oriental rugs made during the past four centuries. They have lavish Oriental rug magazines to draw on, auction catalogues with scores of color plates, and catalogues from rug exhibitions. Many a color plate from Sotheby's auction catalogues has reappeared in a new rug six months later. Technology has helped rugmakers today become extraordinarily sophisticated.

But improvements in travel may be even more important than improvements in information technology. Some Western rugmakers make trips to Pakistan, for instance, every month to supervise their production. Lately I made a buying trip to Pakistan, round trip, in four days. Inexpensive, fast travel has permitted scenarios like the following to take place: An American rugmaker flies to Turkey and arranges to have dyed wool shipped to China;

Egyptian weaver working at an A. Moustafa loom near Cairo, 1998. (Courtesy of Keith DeMare.)

he flies on to China and sees that weavers are off to a proper start making rugs with the Turkish wool before he jogs on to Germany to check up on his European operations; back home in New York, he ships already completed rugs to West Coast retailers, and the rugs arrive there five days later.

Modern communications technology is also important. One American importer who makes rugs in Nepal, aided by fax transmissions and computers, can and does produce and deliver large custom carpets to order in a total of three months or less. Incredible! The rug renaissance exists in a brave new world of technology. Recently I examined a shipment of rugs from Pakistan that had landed in San Francisco. I asked the Afghan importer whether he could get more of a certain type of rug. He said, 'Just a minute,' and took a cellular phone off his hip. A few moments later he said yes, he could get more. He had just phoned his brother in Mazar-e-Sharif. I was astonished. The last time I was in Afghanistan, before the Russian invasion, it was not possible to phone from one end of town to the other. Communications technology has greased the wheels of the renaissance—if you will permit my mixing metaphors.

To summarize, then: The renaissance was stimulated by a renewed interest in Oriental rugs that started in the '60s and increased over the next thirty years. Interest initially focused on antique tribal and village rugs, which were scarce and expensive and unavailable in large sizes. When young American rug dealers living in Turkey were exposed to the pioneering work of German Harald Böhmer, who instituted a production of village rugs with natural dyes in 1980, they loved the idea, ran with it, and essentially perfected it, finally delivering to the market a relatively inexpensive and wholly satisfying alternative to antique rugs. I am calling 1985 the beginning of the renaissance, because it was then that the new tribal and village rugs began to be seen in the markets in America and Europe.

Phase Two of the renaissance also was driven by a strong change in fashions in the rug industry, this time in the direction of decorative carpets. The challenge began to be met by young Americans and Europeans in Nepal in partnership with the Tibetan refugees who had created the carpet industry there. In the process of filling needs in the market, pioneer rugmakers in Turkey and Nepal improved the quality of Oriental rugs: in Turkey by rediscovering the use of twenty-five-hundred year-old technology, in Nepal by experimenting with color and design. The commercial success of the new Turkish and Nepalese rugs started a kind of chain reaction, and dozens and finally hundreds of American rugmakers ventured on interesting new approaches. The renaissance was launched. Rugmakers were aided by the availability of a displaced population of Tibetan weavers in Nepal, a vast number of displaced weavers in Pakistan, and the increased control over production that they enjoyed when India, Pakistan, China, and others filled in for Iran as our major source of rugs. Finally, Western rugmakers and their counterparts in the East were aided by advances in information, transportation, and communications technology. As I've stressed, however, while technology and political change helped the renaissance along, it was the resourceful, adventurous and visionary rugmakers themselves who deserve principal credit for it.

And on it goes. Though the renaissance has passed through its formative stage, it still seems young to me. The techniques of rugmaking, some of which, like natural dyeing and hand spinning, had to be rediscovered, are now in place. The craftspeople are in place—skillful weavers, spinners, and dyers. The market is in place: the public has voted its approval. Now it will be fascinating to watch the renaissance evolve.

New Turkish kilim, in natural dyes and handspun wool. It was imported by Paul Ramsey of Denver, who takes a hand in designing the kilims he imports. (David Holbrook Young.)

A Mahindra, based on an old north Persian Bakshaish. I venture to say that not a single carpet was made in the world from 1930 to 1985 as good as any of these Mahindras.

Folklife rug from Woven Legends. Weavers of rugs like this piece are free to weave almost anything they want. This rug's weaver managed to make an asymmetrical design feel harmonious.

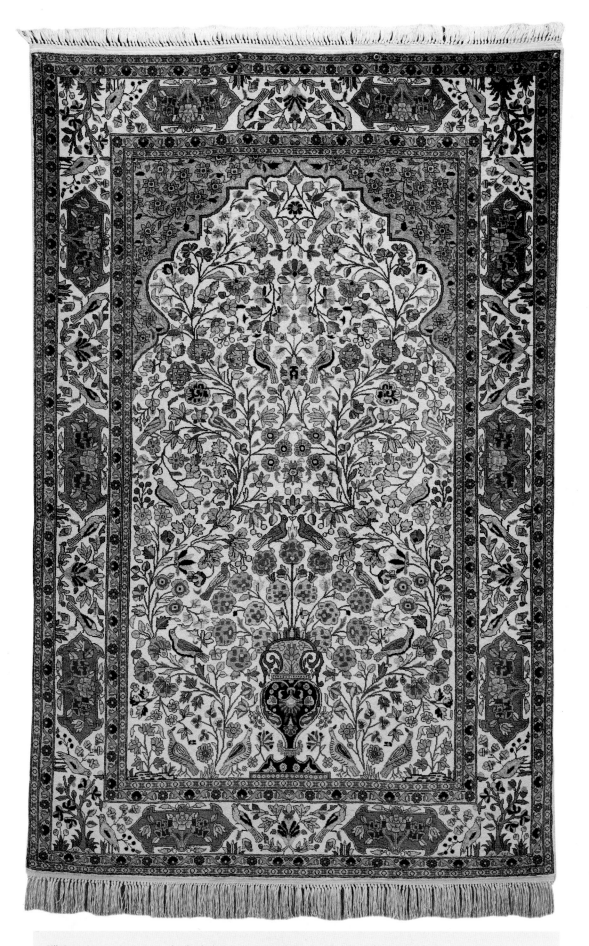

Silk Egyptian rug in a vase and mihrab design. It was made by Nasr N. Salem of Egypt and is about 3' by 5'.

1973 China provisionally granted Most Favored Nation trade status

1976 First International Chinese Carpet Conference

c. 1976 American-born Tombo makes rugs in Nepal with natural dyes under tutelage of Tibetan refugees

c. 1978 Empress of Iran sponsors natural dye project in southern Iran

c. 1978 Harald Böhmer analyzes natural dyes in Turkey

1979 Revolution and hostage crisis in Iran

1979 Soviet Union invades Afghanistan; hundreds of thousands flee

1980 DOBAG established in Turkey; natural dyes reintroduced to weavers

1981 George Jevremovic first sees natural-dyed DOBAG rugs

1982 Chris Walter first sees DOBAG natural-dyed rugs

c. 1983 George Jevremovic produces Azeri prototype

1985 United Nations sponsors natural dye project in Kabul, Afghanistan

1984 or '85 Megerian and Iraj work with natural dyes in Egypt

1985 Natural-dyed rugs from Nepal, Woven Legends, DOBAG, Ayvacik, Konia, Egypt, and a few pieces from southern Iran, begin arriving in the U.S.—and we are calling this the beginning of the renaissance

1986 James Tufenkian begins production of Tibetan rugs in Nepal

1987 Stephanie Odegard begins production of Tibetan rugs in Nepal

1987 Chris Walter establishes Ersari Project and initiates first natural dye enterprise in Pakistan

1990 Chris Walter founds Aryana in Pakistan with Habibullah

1990 Teddy Sumner and George Jevremovic start first natural dye project in India

1990 Chinese government corporation system breaks down; U.S. importers now deal with factories directly

1990 Teddy Sumner and George Jevremovic start first production in China with natural dyes imported from Turkey

1994–1995 Robinson and Samad and their producer achieve nearly perfect finish for decorative carpets in India

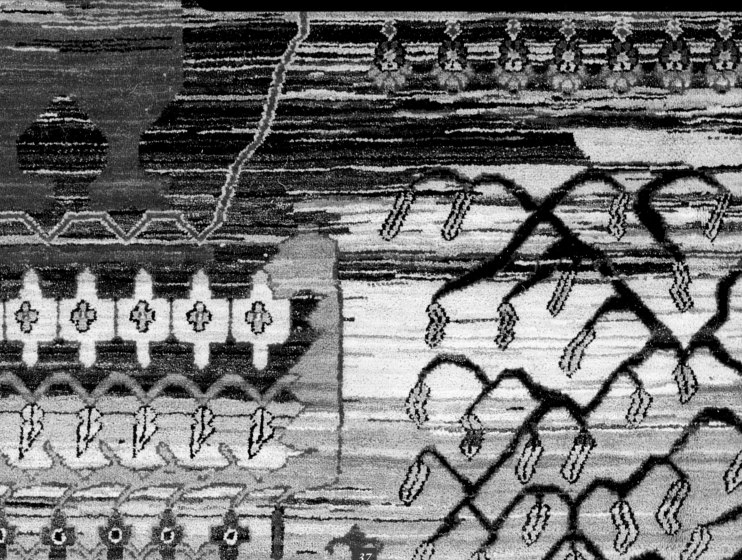

Chapter 2

How Oriental Rugs Are Made Today... And Why Good Rugs Cost Extra

Most books on Oriental rugs describe how Oriental rugs were made in some distant time—without mentioning that what they describe is an idealized model that no longer applies. The men of the family are said to shear lambs of their wool, which the women then weave into rugs, guided in their designs by family tradition. The spinning is supposed to be done by hand. And yet when Teddy Sumner and George Jevremovic wanted to have wool spun by hand in India in 1990, they were lucky eventually to find two or three elderly women who remembered how to do it, only because they had been followers of Mahatma Gandhi, for whom spinning was a kind of mantra. And when they wanted to have wool handspun in China, they had to bring women over from Turkey in order to demonstrate how it was done.

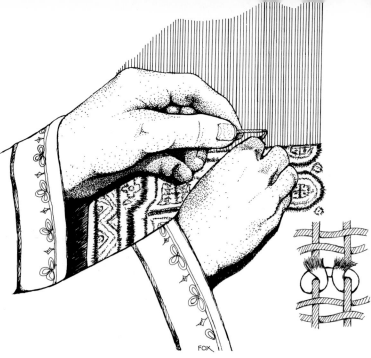

Weavers tie knots around two longitudinal (warp) threads, and the two ends of the knot form the rug's pile. Though the drawing shows what is known as a Turkish or symmetrical knot, is it really a knot? Perhaps it would be better called a 'wrap'. The horizontally running (weft) threads will be beaten down on the knots to keep them from slipping out. Several types of knots are used in Oriental rugs, each associated with a particular ethnic group or area.

A rug manufactory in Lahore, Pakistan, 1998. Even in modern, well-run productions, like this one, Oriental rugs are far from being cranked out on conveyor belts, as one might imagine when words like 'factory' are used to describe their production. In this medieval-looking courtyard, wool is sorted, dyed with natural dyes, and dried; rugs fresh off the loom are clipped, then washed and dried. Edges are flattened, irregularities are corrected. Rugs are inventoried and sent off to market. Dozens of workers, mostly Turkmen in this case, are employed, fed, and housed here as well.

So many of the details and so many of the conditions under which rugs are made today differ so profoundly from the model described in most rug books that it is time to re-examine how rugs are woven—or should I say produced? since weaving is but one step in their production.

Before we look at how rugs are made today, let us look at the techniques that have remained the same for millennia,

the techniques that define what Oriental rugs are. Oriental rugs differ from nearly all others in one important respect: their pile, the part we walk on, is *tied* to the rug's foundation, rather than merely glued to it or passed through the foundation, as is the case with machine-made rugs. That may explain why Oriental rugs last much longer: their pile endures until the rug's foundation is worn through. Weavers tie already dyed pieces of yarn to a rug's foundation by hand, and hence Oriental rugs are known as hand-knotted carpets. In a sense, an Oriental rug is the aggregate of the knots tied in it, for its pile is constituted of the two ends of each knot.

At the same time that weavers are securing the pile material to the foundation, they are also creating designs by alternating the colors of yarns they tie to the foundation. You would be doing something similar if you were to draw a picture by filling in each square of a graph paper with an appropriate color. The tricky part, and one of the features of Oriental rugs that make them what they are, is creating the designs line by line, from one end of the rug (that is, from one of the fringed perimeters) to the other. Imagine that you wish to draw a picture of a boy on a piece of graph paper, but you must do it line by horizontal line, filling in the squares with color. Your first line would consist of the soles of his shoes, the next five rows might be the rest of his shoes, then his ankles, and so on. The last lines of your drawing would consist of his hat. This weaving technique defines what can be done in a rug—or at least done easily and naturally.

The technique of knotting rugs is at least three thousand years old, but there are other methods of making rugs that predate it. The most important is the simple plain weave which produces rugs that are without nap or pile, and are said to be flat-woven. They are made about the same way that I used to weave popsicle sticks together as a child—although they are made on a loom, and they tend to hold up a little better. These rugs, known as kilims (ki LEEM), are made by interweaving longitudinal threads called the warp and transverse threads called the weft on a loom.

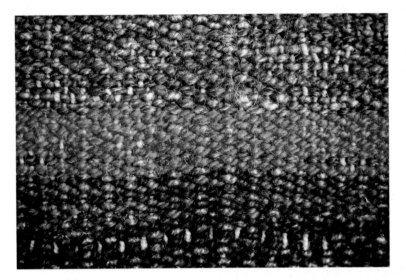

Close-up view of a plain-weave kilim. The decorative threads—that is, the ones intended to be seen—run horizontally across the kilim and are called wefts. However, the white warp threads, which theoretically should be covered by the wefts, are visible here and there. They run vertically.

When the technique for making knotted rugs developed several thousand years ago, it was a breakthrough. Not only did it result in sturdier rugs, it allowed for a much higher degree of ornamentation than was possible with earlier techniques such as felting, a process of binding wool together by wetting it and forcing the fibers to shrink and adhere to one another as they dry.

As I have said, the traditional model of how rugs are made is obsolete. What follows is an account of how rugs are most often woven today.

Most of the rugs and carpets that enter the U.S. are made by weavers who are under contract to produce rugs in designs and sizes specified by Western importers. These importers may be more or less involved in the details of production. But let us assume that *you* are a Western importer and that you are one of the relative few who are involved in every phase of the rugmaking process.

Consider, first, the problem of *what* to make. No village or family tradition exists to help you decide. Are you, a manufacturer, going to design a rug from your own imagination? Almost certainly not. You would have to be a very unusual person to be capable of pulling a successful design out of thin air. You are much more likely to search books and magazines for photographs of the best rugs you can find, guided as well, of course, by your judgment of what will be fashionable when your rugs come off the loom. In this case, let us say that you own an antique Ferahan Sarouk and believe that a reproduction of it would sell well—if you really could capture its wonderful grace. You begin to consider the matter of color. It is axiomatic in the Oriental rug business that color is what sells a rug. In fact you are not quite comfortable with the field color of your old Sarouk. It seems a bit too pink, and you decide that in your production the field color should be deeper and darker. You select a bit of commercial yarn that you believe is the right color for the field and you save it to show to the dyer later. Now it is time to analyze the construction of your old Ferahan Sarouk. You find that it was made with a Persian knot (open to the left) on a cotton foundation; its weft is blue, and two wefts pass between each row of knots. It has a fully depressed warp and 200 knots per square inch. In fact, there are many other such details to be analyzed concerning how the edges are wrapped, the ends finished, and so on. Now, the question is, given the structure of the rug, who can weave it? Can Afghan weavers in Pakistan handle the technical requirements? You confer with producers in Pakistan and find that your rug is a bit finer than what is usually woven there, but for extra money it can be done. You contract to have a number of pieces (as rug people call rugs) woven, and the producer makes plans to devote a number of looms to your project. But first, you must provide him with a number of important things before work can commence. The first is a drawing of the rug, knot for knot, made on graph paper. This is a job for a specialist and it takes significant time. You will need a different drawing for each size of rug you intend to make. In the meantime, you have calculated how much wool you will require, and you have asked an agent to comb the markets for the best available, for which you will be forced to pay a significant premium. He may well have to go to Afghanistan to find it and more or less smuggle it into Pakistan. Most likely he will find a number of different types of wool, and knowing that each type produces different effects in a carpet, you will have to decide which kind is appropriate for your rug. You must then commission to have the wool carded, a process in which individual strands of wool are separated. Then you must have it spun into strands, or yarn. Since you are reproducing an antique rug, you must have the wool spun by hand, for which you will pay steeply. At the same time, you must find suitable cotton for the foundation, and that must be spun by hand as well, at extra cost. Since you are making rugs that you hope will look like your old Ferahan, you must darken the fringe to give it an antique appearance, and you elect to do that before the rugs are woven. After some discussion you authorize the producer to use a simple tea bath to darken the fringe. Of course,

Dyer working with natural dyes in an Afghan refugee camp in Pakistan. (Mason Purcell.)

you must also have the wool that will go into the pile of the rugs dyed with natural substances if they are to look as good as the original rug, and a specialist must be commissioned who is able to make the exact shade of red you have decided on (and of course all the other colors as well). Few dyers can do this. His esteemed services cost extra.

Now that you have a drawing and the right materials, the producer is ready to string the looms and begin work. The producer is an astute person who is absolutely indispensable. For starters, he knows whether your rug must be made on a vertical or horizontal loom (horizontal, in this case, since the weavers are Turkmen), how to calculate the number, size, and spacing of warp threads to be strung, and just how tightly he may string them without distorting the loom. He also knows which weavers are skillful enough to weave finer-than-average rugs. Master weavers are no less deft at their jobs than the producer. The weavers (all of whom, at your insistence, are 14 years old or older) begin tying knots, following the design you have provided. Heaven forbid that you should run out of dyed wool during this time. If that were to happen, no one could wait while you have new yarn dyed, and, anyway, other people are clamoring to hire away your weavers for projects of their own. If you do run out of dyed wool and work stops, the producer is liable to cut the unfinished rugs off the looms and say, 'Here.' Fortunately you have planned well,

A Turkmen weaver on a horizontal loom. Haripur Refugee Camp, 1989. (Chris Walter.)

and work proceeds. As the weaving draws to a conclusion, you must make certain that the producer understands that you do not want the finished edges of the rug to be perfectly straight. They must be pleasantly (but not radically) irregular if they are to look like your old Ferahan Sarouk.

When the rugs leave the loom, they are extremely thick, having had only a preliminary clipping, and—no getting around it—they look brand new. They still must be clipped and finished. Clipping is especially hard, though, because you have chosen to use handspun wool. The traditional method of clipping handspun wool is to clip it in stages: up to six separate clippings with washings in between. The easy way to handle this problem is to wash the rugs in a kind of conditioner that untangles the fibers of handspun wool. With this treatment, the rugs need only be clipped twice, with one intermediate washing. You believe that the conditioning process harms the wool, and

Turkmen using an electric clipper. It is equipped with a vacuum to pull off clipped wool. Lahore, 1998.

you decide that the rugs must be clipped without conditioner at a far greater cost. None of the washing involves chemicals except soap because you are unwilling to compromise the wool. The long process of cleaning and clipping is interrupted several times by 'load sharing', during which electric power is suddenly cut off in your part of town for mysterious reasons.

After the final clipping, you have a number of attractive rugs, but they do not yet look like antiques. You absolutely will not use harsh chemicals on them to simulate age. What are you going to do to impart the wonderful look of an old, well-used rug? Here we enter an area that will require experimentation and luck. After all, you want your rugs to have the same look as your old Ferahan Sarouk, and there is no formula for that. You will have to be resourceful. So you experiment first on one rug by clipping its pile quite short. But the surface is too regular after the first round of clippings, so you have the rug clipped a little unevenly to simulate natural wear. This helps, but it still does not have the patina of your old Sarouk. Your producer suggests an 'herbal wash', a solution composed of tea and henna (a natural red dye). You are lucky. The wash succeeds in imparting a nice old-rug look, and you are ready to finish the rest of the rugs that have come off the loom in the same manner.

And that is how rugs are most often made today, or rather that is how the best rugs are made—though of course there are any number of variations. There is not much that is romantic about the process, but it involves a very high degree of skill and industry on the part of many craftspeople, plus the vision of one person who sees the process through from beginning to end.

Great rugs, then, cost extra to make. Corners can be cut at every step of the way, and often are. We see the results in the mediocre rugs that clutter many rug stores. I have enormous respect for anyone who can make an exceptional carpet. Only a small minority of the people who import rugs can claim to be rugmakers. Most simply buy goods in India, for instance, and negotiate an arrangement to be the sole distributor of a particular line of rug. They may give that line their company name, but they had no part in making them. What they do is honorable and difficult, but it is not rugmaking. Many Easterners and a handful of Westerners are rugmakers. Jack Simantob is a rugmaker. Mason Purcell is a rugmaker. Chris Walter, Teddy Sumner, George Jevremovic, and a small number of other Americans are rugmakers as well. They design, they ride herd on their looms, they gather supplies,

Rug washers and senior staff members in a Lahore manufactory, 1998.

they keep child labor out of their productions, they insist on things being done exactly the way they want. In some cases they learn to speak the language of the weavers, live much of their lives in rough conditions, and suffer exotic diseases and parasites. That so many of today's rugs are so good is especially surprising when we consider that many of the people making rugs today have not had the benefit of learning the old rugmaking skills at their mother's knees. Rugmakers have had to experiment and innovate and learn from scratch. My hat is off to the manufacturers, of course, but also to the dyers, spinners, weavers, designers, producers, graph makers, clippers, washers, as well as the people who repair mistakes, uncurl edges, and straighten crooked rugs.

For many years, Indian rugs were boring. They're not boring any more. This detail of a Mahindra rug from Black Mountain Looms is full of fun, and packed with natural dyes.

Chapter 3

Controversial Issues about New Rugs

Old Rugs versus New

Collectors of old rugs don't like new Oriental rugs, or haven't until recently, and if they like them now, it is only with reluctance. Interior designers have a similar attitude. They are preoccupied with a 'look', and they associate that look with old rugs. But they are pragmatic, and I believe that exposure to the excellent new rugs of this era (and the color plates in this book) will convince many designers that new rugs have to be considered—especially in light of their relatively low price tag.

Collectors of old rugs are the ones I worry about. One, a well-known architect, has recorded his belief that Oriental rugs really haven't amounted to much since the fourteenth century. More indulgent collectors have allowed that Oriental rugs had merit until as recently, even, as

A newly completed kilim and Turkish villagers, 1985. (Chris Walter.)

the late nineteenth century. We have seen that, until just a few years ago, they had a point. Collectors could name objective differences (besides age) between antique and new rugs. But now many new rugs again are made with natural dyes and handspun wool, and are fashioned with exactly the same roots and fruits and nuts and knots and wool as rugs made two thousand five hundred years ago. Yet old-rug collectors do not eagerly embrace them. What are the problems with new rugs...or with old-rug collectors? What are the issues? Let's survey them.

Argument for old rugs: Old Oriental rugs sprang from village traditions and are personal expressions of the weavers who made them. They are real, they are genuine, they are works of art. New rugs, on the other hand, are nothing more than commodities ordered by New York wholesalers.

Response of a new rug advocate: Rug dealers, especially those selling antique carpets, have been masters at promoting the 'noble savage' myth, in which unspoiled weavers in isolated tribes and villages were left alone to pass along design traditions for thousands of years, untainted by commercialism. Even sophisticated rug collectors, I think, have trouble ridding themselves of romantic notions about the cultural purity of the past. But rarely, if ever, has rugmaking been divorced from commerce. Families have always poured into the nearest towns on market day to cash in their carpets. And why not? Are we so certain that whatever has commercial value has any less artistic merit? One could argue just the opposite: that a weaver working on a rug she will sell will make a special effort to do a good job. In fact, many of the ninety-year-old carpets so valued by collectors and interior designers today were strictly commercial productions. Ziegler Mahals (Sultanabads), for instance, were designed and commissioned by a European firm, and Serapis were commissioned by Tabriz rug merchants who, in many cases, supplied designs for Heriz district weavers.

Argument for old rugs: I see new rugs I like, but they are just copies of antique rugs. With both traditional old rugs and new copies of them in the marketplace, which would you rather collect, old rugs or new copies?

Response of a new rug advocate: I would rather collect good rugs, old or new. A connoisseur finds beauty wherever it is: in a fragment of a 12th-century rug, or in a 1995 Little River rug from Black Mountain Looms. But why is it that you call the new rug a copy while you refer to an old village rug as 'traditional'? That village rug is traditional because it is a copy of a copy of a copy—ad infinitum. You may say that each village weaver adds something of herself to the rug she copies, but so do today's rugmakers: a different texture, different colors, a different finish. I don't believe I've ever seen a new version of an old rug that hasn't changed in some important way. Some are successful, and some are not. The trick is to separate the wheat from chaff. That is half the fun of selecting an Oriental rug.

Argument for old rugs: Almost everyone acknowledges that Oriental rugs become more beautiful as they grow older. There seems to be something about age itself that contributes to the beauty of rugs and carpets. Washing new rugs with chemicals simply cannot duplicate the natural beauty that comes from time.

Response of a new rug advocate: Oh, I don't know. I have seen respected, professional rug dealers who specialize in antique carpets (I could name names) mistake brand new Oriental rugs for pieces ninety years old—and offer to buy them! If it is age that gives old rugs their character, how do you account for experts being fooled by rugs with no age at all? I have come to believe that it is use rather than age which accounts for the admittedly appealing character of old rugs. Use can be simulated in new rugs without compromising their wool. Anyway, even if no effort is made to 'age' a new rug, it will become an old rug soon enough. After all, even the oldest rug began life as a newborn. On the question of whether it is age or use that gives rugs a pati-

Detail of a new Aryana with an East Turkestan design. It is not uncommon even for experts to mistake rugs like this for antiques. And why not? It was made almost exactly the way rugs were made 2500 years ago.

The design of this carpet may be used more than once, but its colors, produced in small batches of natural dyes, will vary so greatly from one rug to the next that no two rugs will ever look alike. It was made in India by Rugs by Robinson of Atlanta, Georgia.

na, consider the Armenian immigrant rugs. These rugs flowed by the thousands into America during the years surrounding 1990, brought by Armenian immigrants upon the breakup of the Soviet Union. These rugs were fairly old, some dated as early as 1915, but many had been mounted on walls in Armenia during most of their lives and hence were essentially unused and in nearly perfect condition. Collectors found these rugs 'too new', but I believe they really found them too unused. Ironically, to make these old pieces more desirable to collectors, an enterprising rug dealer would have to lay these nearly perfectly preserved Armenian immigrant rugs out in the streets for three months and beat them up until they matched the expectations rug collectors have of how old rugs are supposed to appear. It is interesting to compare the disappointment many art lovers felt when the ceiling of the Sistine Chapel was cleaned, exposing disturbingly bright colors in Michelangelo's paintings.

Argument for old rugs: Old rugs were one-of-a-kind. New rugs are cranked out like automobiles: there may be different models, but rugs of each model are alike as peas in a pod.

Response of a new rug advocate: Some rugs made today are, as you say, cranked out and nearly identical. Of course the same was true eighty years ago. Caucasian rugs, Turkmen rugs, Persian village rugs, Turkish village rugs—thousands were so alike that they may as well have been identical. Actually, some rugs in the market now are one-of-a-kind: certain rugs made by Samad Brothers and Rugs by Robinson, for instance. Their designs may be repeated, but their colors vary so greatly because of their small-batch dyeing and the use of natural dyes that for all practical purposes there will never be another like them. Other productions, such as Woven Legends, allow weavers so much freedom to improvise elements of design that their rugs are never exactly alike. This one-of-a-kind approach is one of the aspects of new-rugmaking that I find revolutionary.

Argument for old rugs: Rugmakers have succeeded in making new rugs look good through technical accomplishments such as learning how to use natural dyes, but mostly by copying the look of old rugs. How much real creativity is there in modern Oriental carpets? Compare what today's rugmakers are doing with what artisans did in sixteenth-century Persia during the Safavid dynasty. Then we had an artistic revolution; today we have a technical renaissance.

Response of a new rug advocate: We agree that this is in part a technical renaissance, but we make no apology for that. Before about 1980, natural dyeing and the practice of spinning wool by hand were essentially dead. Unlike Safavid-era artisans, modern rugmakers had to learn the craft from scratch. It is astonishing that they have accomplished so much, especially considering how tempting it must have been to continue working with the excellent, inexpensive, modern synthetic dyes at their disposal. That is a temptation Safavid rugmakers did not have to overcome.

But about creativity. Were the Safavids more creative than today's rugmakers? They certainly had more resources at their disposal—the resources of the Persian court. They could afford to educate and employ specialists whose only job was to design rugs. They could afford the finest wool and dyestuffs imaginable. They could afford to employ the best weavers in the world. They could afford to work on one palace-sized piece with 500 knots per square inch for years. And they could afford not to sell the carpet when it was completed. I wonder if we mistake the exceptional advantages Safavid weavers enjoyed for exceptional creativity.

But creativity is a tricky matter in a conservative medium like Oriental carpets—or the blues. If a blues singer is to be taken seriously, he has to sound like a blues singer. His first concern is to sound authentic. Likewise, whoever aspires to be an Oriental rugmaker must make rugs that look like Oriental rugs. A rug weaver is in a bind. Today, if she copies other rugs, she is not considered creative. If she is too creative, she is not making Oriental rugs.

Rugmakers now are doing about what rugmakers have always done. Most look around to see what everybody else is making. Fortunately, a lot of people today are making interesting pieces, and others jump in and find interesting things to do, too. But then there are a few individuals who go beyond that. They are the truly gifted, and perhaps they are geniuses in their fields. I will name my candidates, though I fear I will embarrass them, while making enemies of dozens of other excellent rugmakers whom I slight

Not much real creativity in today's Oriental rugs? This carpet, a Kentwilly from Black Mountain Looms, had its genesis when the publisher of Rug News, Leslie Stroh, asked Teddy Sumner of Black Mountain Looms to make a rug for his family. Mr. Stroh had some ideas of his own, and, in time-honored tradition, began the design process by going to book-cover designs for inspiration. But instead of searching through Safavid period book-covers, as Safavid designers would have done, he went to Alphonse Mucha, a pioneer artist in the Art Nouveau style at the turn of the century, and found elements from book plates that he liked. He cut and pasted this and that from a Dover book until he had a pleasing pastiche. Teddy Sumner (a painter, by the way) took it from there. He changed a little, re-scaled, refined, and did much more before the design became a carpet. About four years later, a 10 by 20-foot carpet came off the loom. Now, was the design of this rug creative or not? You may draw your own conclusion, but I am decided in my opinion that, though the co-designers used elements drafted a century earlier, what they did was creative from beginning to end. In the final analysis, they created something that was unlike any carpet that had ever before existed—something new and wonderful. They are far from alone in being creative rug designers at the beginning of the twenty-first century. (Don Tuttle.)

unfairly. They are Teddy Sumner, George Jevremovic, and Chris Walter. I suspect there are native producers of whom I am unaware who belong in this small group, and I am certain that other people in the rug industry will have worthy candidates of their own. Other rugmakers have made rugs as good as the best of the people I have mentioned, but the breadth and extent of their accomplishments set these three apart. (You can find more about them in Part Two.) All are grounded in traditional design: George Jevremovic and Chris Walter in antique Oriental rugs, Teddy Sumner more in Western design. But from their grounding in tradition has come something special, something—yes—creative. This indeed is a period of creative rugmaking. The renaissance goes far beyond technical advances, and I am confident that when collectors a hundred years from now sort out the rugs and carpets of our era, many will be found to have withstood the test of time. I think future collectors will have no hesitation at all in proclaiming many of our contemporary rugs works of art.

Argument for old rugs: Antique rugs are proven survivors. They have been exposed to sunlight, they've been washed and walked on, they have been tried and tested by use. If you buy an antique rug that looks good, you can be pretty certain there will be no surprises. Of course that is not true of new rugs.

Response of a new rug advocate: I agree.

The irony inherent in the old rug/new rug argument, of course, is that, long before the argument is settled, new rugs will be old rugs, and then, I trust, they will get some respect! In the meantime, new rugs are much less expensive than old ones that are in good condition, and that is a powerful and sometimes deciding argument in their favor. Having spent decades on the floor, antique rugs can be tricky to buy. They may contain old repairs, stains, and rotten areas, and they may even have been painted to hide wear. New rugs are much easier to buy with confidence.

How do I feel personally about new rugs vs. old? The truth is that I find new rugs every day that I love, and then, from time to time, I find an antique rug that just completely staggers me. Something *does* happen to Oriental rugs with use over time. George Jevremovic compares rugs with certain kinds of African art objects whose makers 'empower' them by various rituals. Oriental rugs, he says, are empowered by use. There is truth in what he says. Unaccountably, after they have been danced on, spilled on, wet on, and lived on by families for generations, they seem to look better. New rugs will similarly improve over time.

The first rug I ever owned may have been the best one I will *ever* own. It was a Tekke main carpet, probably 150 years old, with the quintessential Tekke red. Those were my boot days, and I wore the rug out in about three years. I will never again use an antique carpet on the floor. Thank God for new rugs that we know are improving—rather than starting to decline—with continued use.

Natural Dyes and Synthetic Dyes

We have seen that one of the 'revolutionary' aspects of modern rug production has been the return of natural dyes. Not long ago, shoppers who were interested in new rugs (or who couldn't or wouldn't spend the money to buy antiques or semi-antiques) had no choice but to buy rugs with synthetic dyes. Today, though, natural dyes are an option in new rugs and, in fact, you will have to decide between natural and synthetic dyes if you buy one. The choice is important because, aside from everything else, natural-dyed rugs cost roughly 30 percent more than synthetic-dyed rugs. Let's look closely at synthetic and natural dyes and how they compare.

You will find that I use several words for natural dyes: 'natural', 'vegetal', and 'vegetable'. I prefer 'natural', but use the others simply because I get tired of typing out 'natural' time after time. 'Vegetal' and 'vegetable' are slightly misleading because one natural dye, cochineal, is made from an insect and is not vegetal at all. Once a manufacturer of Turkish kilims told me proudly that she makes her rugs from 'organic' dyes. I seemed to remember from high-school chemistry that 'organic' refers to any material that is carbon-based, and I questioned her closely about organic dyes. She admitted that she bought the dyes from a Swiss dye maker. I'm still not clear what 'organic' dyes are, exactly, but something tells me that they are not mixed from roots.

Rugmakers of the Middle East and Asia have used natural dyes for thousands of years. In the classic model, weaving is done most often by women and dyeing most often by men. In some important rug-weaving areas of the Middle East, dyers make reds from dried, ground madder root and (less often) from cochineal, blues from indigo, yellow from weld, green from sequential dyeing in indigo and weld, brown and camel from walnut husks, other colors from many other vegetal substances. Every area has its own indigenous materials from which dyes are made. Some dyeing takes place in two steps. First, in a process called 'mordanting', yarn is dipped into a hot solution of alum or iron, which prepares wool fibers to bond permanently with dye. Then the yarn is placed in vats of hot dye where it is cooked for shorter or longer periods of time and at higher or lower temperatures, depending on the dye and the shade desired. Natural dyes are expensive in the sense that they take a lot of time: time to pick or dig up, time to dry, grind, and finally seep. Some, like natural indigo, must be dyed repeatedly to obtain permanence. But when vegetal dyes have been handled correctly, the colors they produce are wonderful. Colors are usually

Wool seeping in a pot of madder dye in Lahore, 1998.

saturated without being edgy or harsh. They seem to glow. Even in skeins of yarn not yet woven, naturally produced colors are simply beautiful. One writer (Reinhard G. Hubel, *The Book of Carpets*, New York 1970) suggests that Persian weavers do not really deserve their reputation for having a wonderful sense of color, because, with such gorgeously colored, naturally dyed yarns at their disposal, no weaver could possibly go wrong using any combination of colors in a rug! Ironically, natural dyes often strike people as too bright, except in a rug that has been walked on for decades or washed to soften its colors. Fortunately, natural dyes, if they are well made to begin with, age beautifully. Colors soften without essentially changing. (Early synthetics often changed colors with age: from a bright purple to gray, for instance.) And, if anything, colors become even more lustrous with use on the floor.

Perhaps the most charming effect of natural dyes is a certain variegated look they produce in a rug, adding character to it and helping to keep it from feeling static. This is most easily seen in natural greens, which show flecks of blue and yellow (from which green is composed). But a close look at most rugs with natural dyes will show you that none of the colors is quite uniform. Why is that? Part of the phenomenon is due to the irregularities of handspun wool (as we shall see), which is often used along with natural dyes; and partly to the association of natural dyes with small productions in which only tiny lots of dye are mixed at any one time, each of which is slightly different from the others. Furthermore, natural dyes are a bit transparent because they are not absorbed by wool as thoroughly as synthetic dyes; hence the color of the wool shows through the dye and adds to the variegated look. The net effect of all this pleasing irregularity of color is a rug that is vibrant, never mechanical-feeling: it gives an impression of character.

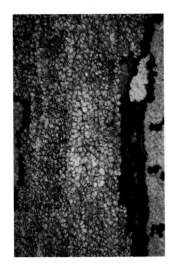

This variegated green shows specks of blue and yellow, ordinarily a sign of natural dyes. The other colors are variegated too, but more subtly.

As far as practical considerations are concerned, by and large natural dyes, as they are handled by rugmakers in the Middle East, are phenomenally stable. Museum collections contain 400-year-old rugs whose colors are almost unbelievably vibrant. They resist fading in sunlight and they resist running when exposed to water. In other practical respects though, natural dyes do have drawbacks. They can't produce certain colors that can be made with synthetics. Natural dyes that are used to make dark brown often oxidize and cause wool to break down prematurely. Vegetal dyes can also be faulted for being expensive, hard to work with, and time-consuming. For rugmakers wishing to produce rugs 'in continuity' (that is, a number of different rugs in all sizes, with absolutely consistent colors) natural dyes are impossible because results are inconsistent and unpredictable.

Synthetic dyes were invented in the 1860s, and a class of dyes known as aniline was in use in the Middle East in rugs by 1900. The early synthetics were wretched things that nearly ruined the Oriental rug industry. A perhaps-apocryphal story, repeated in probably every rug book written in the last seventy-five years, has it that at one time a law was made in Iran banning the use of synthetic dyes, at the cost of the miscreant's right hand. But the use of anilines of course continued. Some early synthetics bled when exposed to water, others faded radically, some changed colors with age, and certain colors (notably a vile harsh orange) never lost its hard-as-nails edge. We would all be better off, I suspect, if, when considering synthetic dyes in new rugs, we could simply forget about the failures of these early anilines. Our dislike for them should never extend to the next generation of synthetics, which are far superior. We would also be better off if we could forget our almost universal prejudice toward anything 'synthetic'. The word carries a pejorative connotation unfair to the synthetic dyes currently in use.

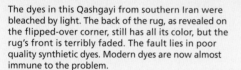

The dyes in this Qashgayi from southern Iran were bleached by light. The back of the rug, as revealed on the flipped-over corner, still has all its color, but the rug's front is terribly faded. The fault lies in poor quality synthietic dyes. Modern dyes are now almost immune to the problem.

Synthetic dyes. These are especially bad synthetic dyes, but they serve to make a point. This red is edgy, harsh, too bright. The orange has a similar quality.

Synthetic dyes, but pleasant. These are modern chrome dyes tastefully chosen and expertly used. Sometimes it is impossible to distinguish between good synthetic and natural dyes. Still, compare the green in this with the green in the natural dye sample. Here it lacks variegation.

This new class of dyes was in use in the Middle East by around 1940. Mordanted with potassium bichromate, they are known as chrome dyes. They have now been in use for more than fifty years and are nearly perfect. They are cheap and easy to use. They produce an enormous range of consistent colors that are fast in water, resistant to fading, and non-corroding to wool. It is often said (especially by old-rug fanciers) that chrome dyes are too good, that they are so unyielding to light and time that they will never soften and acquire the mellow patina so esteemed in antiques. As a dealer who has washed rugs for the past twenty-nine years, I have had an excellent opportunity to observe how rugs of all kinds, including those with chrome dyes, have aged. The news is good. I've been surprised to find that almost all those made with chrome dyes in the past fifteen years or so come back from washing looking very lustrous. Their colors have softened in a pleasant way. I would single out Indian rugs as aging especially nicely, and Romanian rugs as well. Nearly all rugs with chrome dyes are growing older just as we like them to. (I am less happy with chrome-dyed rugs of a slightly

earlier period. Certain Persian rugs of the '70s have showed disturbing tendencies to fade even in weak, indirect sunlight.) One complaint natural-dye enthusiasts voice about Oriental rug colors crafted from synthetic dyes is true, though. They do not have the variegation natural dyes impart. For instance, no synthetic green has the 'flecky' character of a natural green. Is that important? That's a call you will have to make.

Now, having spent some time pointing out the differences between natural and synthetic dyes, I have to admit that quite often it is impossible even for an expert to tell the difference between them without chemical analysis. Yes, there are certain colors from early dyes that are clearly synthetic: I have mentioned a particularly irritating orange. But modern chrome dyes are another matter. How can you tell the difference between them and natural dyes? Sometimes you can't, short of sending samples to a laboratory for analysis. Even experts often disagree as to whether a particular dye in a rug is natural or synthetic.

Turkmen woman spinning wool with a drop spindle.

Spinning is the process of twisting together and drawing out massed short fibers into a continuous strand. The technique of spinning wool by hand has been known for some thousands of years, and was in exclusive use for preparing the wool that constitutes the pile of a rug until the invention of machines for the purpose. Spinning wool was an almost unceasing activity for girls and women in rugmaking cultures. Women would spin whenever they were free to do so, even while they walked. It is not surprising that, when machines were invented for spinning wool, rugmakers abandoned their traditional methods. We can surmise that some village and tribal rugmakers continued to spin wool by hand, but by World War II nearly all wool used in city-made rugs was spun by machine. Strangely, I don't recall that the subject of hand versus machine spinning was ever spoken of or written about by rug experts during the 1970s and '80s, which were my first twenty years in the rug business. I first heard the subject mentioned in about 1985 when a San Francisco rug dealer boasted that a new production of rugs he was carrying (in retrospect I think they must have been Ayvaciks from Turkey) were made with handspun wool. That startled me. Until then, I must have assumed that all rugs were made with handspun wool. I was wrong. In fact, most Oriental rugs have been made with machine-spun wool since about 1945.

The distinction between hand- and machine-spun wool is far from academic. The wool we are speaking of is the material used for the pile of a rug; for all practical purposes, it *is* the rug. Handspun and machine-spun wool have different properties that crucially affect how a rug looks. Handspun wool yarn is irregular in the tension of its twist; it is inadvertently spun looser in some places and tighter in others. One practical effect of this irregularity is that, when soaked in dye, handspun yarn absorbs less where it is spun tightly and more where it is spun loosely. Without perhaps meaning to, the spinners have created yarn that, when dyed, is never uniform in color. Another practical effect of the lack of uniformity is a slightly uneven, 'nubby' surface on the rug. Because of these two factors—the irregularity of colors, and the rug's irregular texture—such carpets have a very handmade look.

I am becoming aware of a problem that purchasers of rugs with handspun wool sometimes encounter. During the first months of using them, owners notice that loose ends of the pile are pulled up by vacuuming. Pieces of pile stick up a half-inch to an inch above the rest of the pile. All rugs have this problem when they are new, though it is clearly more pronounced in carpets with handspun pile. Though it can be scary to rug owners, the phenomenon is harmless. The loose ends of pile can be and should be clipped the same height as the rest of the pile. If proper care has not been taken by the rugmaker in the clipping, the situation can, on rare occasions, be annoying enough to be considered a real problem—though one that affects the appearance of a carpet, never its longevity.

Even though handspun wool is seen much more often today than even a few years ago, it still is found in only a small minority of new rugs. I know of no source for hard information about this, but I estimate that perhaps 3 percent of today's production is handspun.

Machine-spun (sometimes referred to as mill-spun) wool in an Oriental rug looks quite different from handspun wool—at least in new rugs. (I believe, though I'm not certain, that, as rugs age and the pile is loosened with use, the difference between the two becomes less apparent.) Because the tension of its spin is so uniform, machine-

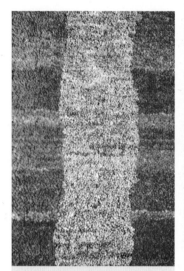 

Handspun wool absorbs dye unevenly and produces variegated color. It has an uneven, nubby surface. This creates an informal, hand-made look in carpets.

Machine-spun wool absorbs dye evenly. Color is uniform and the surface of a machine-spun wool rug is even.

spun wool absorbs dye evenly, and colors are more consistent. And because of the uniformity of the tension in machine-spun yarn, a rug made with it will have a very regular and finished look. You will easily be able to see the differences in handspun rugs and machine-spun rugs if you examine them side by side and look for the differences I have described.

Now, which is right for you, a rug made from handspun or one from machine-spun wool? The considerations are so tied to considerations about natural vs. synthetic dyes that it is best to discuss them together—which we do below.

Natural dyes and handspun wool in an Aryana from Yayla Tribal Rugs. It lies on the floor in my study, and I draw inspiration from it every day.

For all practical purposes, both natural dyes and modern chrome dyes are superb, and so are hand- and machine-spun wool. I believe that the choices one has to make among them are strictly personal and aesthetic. There are four ways in which they may be combined: natural dye with handspun wool; natural dye with machine-spun wool; synthetic dye with handspun wool; and synthetic dye with machine-spun wool. Let us consider each of them in turn.

If you like the homespun look of tribal and village rugs, with lots of color variegation and other elements that add up to an impression of character, you are almost certain to be attracted to rugs made with handspun wool. Once you have been shown the difference between it and machine-spun wool in a rug, you will have no trouble telling them apart. Most likely you will also prefer the look of natural dyes to synthetic, though the difference between them is not as apparent. Generally, natural dyes will add to the pleasant irregularities that attract those who prefer tribal to city rugs. The combination of natural dyes and hand-spun wool is time-honored—used for more than 2500 years

(that we know of). The extra cost of each is worth the expense to some, if for no reason other than the mere tradition of their use together. But it is the unparalleled character imparted by natural dyes and handspun wool in combination that makes it my own clear personal favorite.

However, handspun wool so greatly enhances the texture and appearance of most rugs that one may find that, for some, the use of natural dyes on top of handspun wool pile pays only diminishing esthetic returns and is an unnecessary expense. Both George Jevremovic and Teddy Sumner, important producers of handspun, natural-dyed rugs, have told me that, in their opinion, handspun wool is the more important of the two—and I agree. There are relatively few rugs made with handspun wool and synthetic dyes except for Tibetan rugs (many of which have this combination). Most people would agree that the colors and texture of the best of these Tibetan rugs look great (see Chapter Five).

People who prefer the finished, formal look of city rugs are likely to be attracted to rugs with machine-spun wool

Handspun wool and synthetic dyes in a Tibetan rug from Endless Knot Rug Company. Except in Tibetan rugs, this is an unusual combination though it makes perfect sense. Endless Knot makes some of the best contemporary designs in the market. This is an original design by Amy Choi called Sentarsa.

and synthetic dyes. Certainly those who are meticulous about order and regularity, and who admire symmetry and perfection, will gravitate toward these rugs. Typically, they have colors and surfaces of great consistency. They lack abrash and other irregularities that are off-putting to some people. These folks are in luck, because good rugs in chrome dyes and mill-spun pile are in great supply and relative bargains.

There is one last combination to consider: rugs with machine-spun wool and natural dyes. These are among the most successful rugs today, and many sophisticated designers favor them together. In any case, those who weave rugs of this type, like Samad Brothers and Rugs by Robinson, often seem to have the decorative rug market in mind. In a way, this pairing has the best of both worlds: mill-spun yarn is finished-looking enough for the most formal of settings, while natural dyes and their attendant abrash and variegation lend character and personality.

Now that I have laid out the choices in such an orderly fashion, and you, the reader, have perhaps identified your

This Pakistani 'Persian', also called Pakistani 16/18, from Jerry Aziz in New York, perfectly exemplifies rugs with chrome dyes and machine-spun wool pile. It has a finished, formal look, with little or no abrash.

This piece was woven from machine-spun wool that was dyed from natural substances. The natural dyes give it a pleasant irregularity, while the machine-spun wool gives it a uniform surface and a formal feeling. A Samad Brothers carpet, approximately 8' by 12'.

own preference among them, I have to ruin everything by introducing some additional information. Clever people have learned to fake (or simulate, depending on the intention of the producer) both natural dyes and handspun wool. Machines that spin wool can be manipulated (broken, actually) to cause their speeds to vary erratically, causing the yarn they produce to be spun tighter in places and looser in others. That variation in spin, of course, is exactly what gives handspun wool its (up to now) unique advantage. Natural dye is faked by dipping a large quantity of wool into a synthetic dye bath in stages. Imagine a large quantity of yarn wrapped around a wheel: the wheel is lowered into a dye bath of synthetic dyes a little at a time, so that at the end of the process the first yarn to go in has spent (let's say) eight hours in the dye bath, and the last to go in has spent only two. In this way many different shades are produced from a single dye lot, and the natural variegation of vegetal dyes has been simulated. Clever— but confusing to us who thought we had sorted out the issues surrounding natural and synthetic dyes, and hand- versus machine-spun wool. So the outstanding question is how can one tell the difference between what is real and what is faked? There are differences: the real thing simply looks a little better, but the differences are subtle and do not lend themselves to positive identification in a book. I hate to tell you this, but the best answer is that the price of the rug is probably the best indicator. Natural dyes and handspun wool don't come cheaply, and when you see a rug that appears to have both but is quite inexpensive, watch out. Not that there is any tragedy in buying a rug made as I've just described. On the contrary, the price of these rugs is relatively low and they can look great. It's just that you will want to know what you are getting. You may have to trust your rug dealer to help you sort it out.

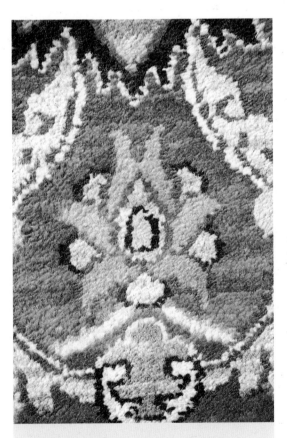

Detail of an inexpensive Indian carpet in which both handspun wool and natural dyes are simulated. The illusion, though good, results in a carpet that lacks depth and liveliness.

An Azeri from Woven Legends. It has been given no chemical treatment at all to age it, nor has its pile been clipped low to suggest age. It is about 8' by 10', colored with natural plant dyes, and woven from handspun wool on a cotton foundation.

Oriental rugs improve with use. Colors soften, the wool pile grows polished and lustrous. Even the nicks and stains old rugs accumulate add character. For at least a hundred years, rug sellers have devised ways to simulate an old-rug look in new rugs, with methods ranging from harmless—to nearly fatal. Some shoppers (and rugmakers) are passionately opposed to the concept of making a new rug look old. Others, like Jack Simantob, the rugmaker/owner of Art Resources in Los Angeles, are more pragmatic. I had voiced concerns to him about what seemed to me to be the high degree of distressing at that time in one line of his rugs. 'You know,' he said, 'it is very important to many people to get just the right look in their homes, especially people with good taste. Not everyone has $25,000 to spend on an antique rug, or sixty years to wait for a new rug to grow old. Even if you have the money to spend, it is not always possible to find the right antique rug. Yes, distressing a rug may take years of useful life out of it, but a new, distressed rug will last at least as long as a $25,000 antique and cost a third as much. As long as people know what they are buying, why not give them what they want, if we can?'

The most widespread method of conferring an older look on new carpets involves washing them in a chemical solution (often involving chlorine) to tone down their colors and add luster. It is a nearly universal practice, and has been for decades. My estimate is that perhaps 90 percent of all rugs and carpets are so treated. Specialists carefully formulate the 'wash', as it is called, aiming at a solution that it is strong enough to impart the softness of age, but not so strong as to corrode wool and radically fade colors. Despite dire warning I have heard and read for nearly thirty years, I have seen no evidence of harm caused by a judicious light wash, and, in fact, a light wash almost always makes carpets look better—better to most people, at least. But every method of making new rugs look old has its extreme. Some rug producers treat their rugs to such caustic chemical baths that the rugs are literally burned. Wool becomes lusterless, colors fade, the surface becomes hazy—rugs seem to die. The practice persists because some consumers demand carpets with a lifeless appearance, strange though that may seem; they are people who care about Oriental rugs only as backdrops for their furniture, and don't wish the carpet to assert itself.

An Indian rug burned by excessive chemicals in the finishing process. Not only do harsh chemicals damage wool and cause premature wear, but often, as in the case of this rug, the chemicals are masking other problems, such as color-run.

But be assured that such radical treatment takes years of useful life away from a rug and ruins its appearance for most people.

Thirty years ago, rugs called Golden Afghans were favored in the American market for a brief while. Kabul merchants created them by pouring battery acid on red Afghan rugs, which instantly turned a 'golden' color. I have not seen any around lately.

Many different kinds of 'washes' are used today, though their formulas are often closely guarded secrets. In the '20s and '30s thousands of rugs were washed in coffee, a natural dye. Today some rugs are washed in tea, another natural dye. An 'herbal' wash is sometimes used; it is a

wash the carpets whose appearance we believe may change with washing before, rather than after, selling them. They always look better for the washing—to us, at least—and no customer will have a nasty surprise the first time they have their rug washed themselves. Let me say clearly, though, that it is unusual for even radically antiqued rugs to change significantly in washing.

Where the technology or materials are not available for 'washing' carpets, for instance in remote Afghan villages, the method of choice for aging them is simply to expose them to the sun. One hilarious ad, sent out by a rug producer some years ago, shows a photo of hundreds and possibly thousands of rugs spread out in the sun. The

An Egyptian carpet to which a slurry of who-knows-what has been added to soften and deepen its colors and impart an antique look.

A finisher blowtorches a carpet to 'age' it. Very often, the backs of rugs are singed to burn off the new-rug fuzz. It is quite another thing to torch the front. As radical as it sounds, however, the carpets thus treated are often quite attractive after being washed.

combination of tea and henna, and I have liked the effect it produces. Sometimes madder, a natural dye, is used in the final wash of an entire rug to 'sadden' it. I am concerned about whether some of these substances are fast in water. We once had occasion to wash an Egyptian rug that had an attractive but rather dark and muddy look when new. After washing, the rug was still attractive, maybe more so than before, but it had changed radically to a bright, cheerful thing. Since then, in my store we

caption reads, 'To insure quality, all our rugs are sun-tested after washing.' (Tested for what?!) The whole aging process is even speedier when weavers spread rugs in the streets for man, beast, machine, and the elements to render them into semi-antiques in a few weeks. They emerge miraculously improved—with a few loose ends, perhaps, but (after washing, of course) with lustrous wool and a pleasant, soft look.

The achievements of rugmakers in the past several years go far beyond techniques merely to soften colors and add a little luster, however. Now some are able to make a new carpet nearly indistinguishable from an old one. Some of the techniques involved sound like torture, but, I must admit, even radical treatments to which I object sometimes make a rug look great. One such treatment involves blow-torching the front and back of a new rug. After it is thus distressed, then cleaned, the result often is a really stunning carpet that appears to be about ninety years old, shows a bit of wear, and needs minor repairs. That description almost perfectly fits antique carpets worth $30,000—and that is just what our distressed new rug is intended to resemble. The new rug, though, sells for $6,000 to $12,000. It is hard to fault the practice when the results are so attractive. Still, you must know, a rug finished in this manner will not live to become an old rug. How long will it last? That depends on how it was aged, the kind of use it takes on the floor, and how it is maintained—but we can guess twenty to thirty-five years (as opposed to sixty-five to one hundred for the same rug not distressed).

A few methods of making rugs look older are unequivocally benign. The most miraculous achievement of modern rug finishing, as far as I am concerned, is the new rug made indistinguishable from a semi-antique rug (in other words, one around fifty years old) without the use of any distressing at all, except, perhaps, a light wash. Instead of making new rugs look like worn antiques, a few manufacturers are content to let them resemble older rugs in good condition. They accomplish this by making a number of good choices. For instance, they choose colors that look like colors found in old rugs, and they weave their rugs in old designs. Using handspun wool and natural dyes helps, and so does an intelligently chosen wash.

A very few rug makers use no aging techniques at all. Woven Legends, a pioneering company in the renais-sance, refuses to use aging of any kind in its Azeri carpets. Woven Legends' preference is for rugs to age naturally, in use on the floor. George Jevremovic of Woven Legends, stubbornly insisted on his no-wash approach until recently, when the decorative rug market swung sharply and decisively toward light, soft colors. He began to 'mess around', as he says, with 'aggressive clipping and so on', and managed to make a new Kentwilly (a rug of his own production) look genuinely old. A friend saw it, approved, and bought the carpet, dropping it into an auction gallery. A group of professional rug dealers, mistaking the rug for an antique, formed a cabal to buy the carpet at auction, which they succeeded in doing—for $27,000. They then held a private auction among themselves, the winner paying some unknown amount greater than that. Not 'aged', the carpet would have sold for around $8,000. It is hard to fault a rug maker for doing 'a little aggressive clipping and so on' when that is what the market wants and the rewards are so great.

One of the ways rugmakers suggest age in new rugs without distressing them is deliberately to introduce abrash into them. Abrash (which I hear pronounced many ways-I pronounce the 'A's' as in apple, and accent the first syllable) occurs naturally when wool is dyed in small batches. The color of each batch differs from the others—sometimes radically. When weavers use up one batch of dyed wool in a rug and begin using the next, bands of different color are created. Abrash suggests age in rugs because abrash was more common before modern large-batch dyeing methods were invented. The effect can be pleasing and can add character to a rug. If too pronounced or if introduced into a rug in which abrash is not appropriate, it can be distracting and mar a rug's looks. Abrash is a matter of personal taste. I often like it, even when it has been introduced deliberately for effect, but I am irritated by it if it seems contrived. You may wish to look for abrash in this book's color plates and develop a sense of how you feel about it.

One Indian producer promotes character and a look of age in his rugs by spinning three strands of differing wool into one yarn. The result, after the wool is dyed, is an interesting carpet whose variegated color and texture suggests age. The procedure is time-consuming and reminds us that creating rugs with character requires real craftsmanship and commitment.

Frankly, I wish rug makers would lighten up on the kinds of antiquing that shorten the life of rugs, even though distressing them may make Oriental rugs look better in the short term. It is not realistic to expect all rug dealers to dissuade people from buying what is attractive to them, and heavily antiqued carpets often are beautiful. Customers buy them without fully understanding that they simply won't last as long as carpets in full pile. It is possible to make rugs look old without damaging them; many producers do just that. But some manufacturers will stop heavily distressing their rugs only when consumers stop buying them. You, rug shoppers, whether you realize it or not, ultimately determine which rugs come to market and how they will be made. Which of the finishes we have spoken of is right for you: no wash, light wash, antique finish, or near-death experience? That is for you to say, of course, but certainly it is worth something, (the price of this book, I hope) to understand your options.

Misconception 1: Old rugs have natural dyes; new rugs have synthetic dyes. Wrong. Most rugs and carpets in the market now that are considered old were made with synthetic dyes. Some new rugs are now made with natural dyes.

Misconception 2: Most new rugs are now made with natural dyes. Wrong. Only about 5 percent of new rugs are made with natural plant dyes. Many people, having heard about natural dyes in new rugs, erroneously assume that they are all made thus. Not true at all.

Misconception 3: Oriental rugs are properly spoken of as carpets, not rugs. In fact, though I often use rug and carpet interchangeably, in the industry, rugs are small, and carpets are those that are bigger than about 6 by 9 feet.

Misconception 4: New carpets with an old look have been given a bath in tea. In fact, that misconception is probably misinformation promoted in the rug trade, including the machine-made rug trade, to put the most benign-sounding spin on rug antiquing. Tea is sometimes used, but almost always in combination with other substances whose effects are permanent.

Misconception 5: Abrash (that is, bands of slightly different color running across a rug) is a sign of natural dyes. In fact, abrash is a sign that wool has been dyed in small batches, each batch being slightly different in shade. But the dyes may be either natural or synthetic. Often abrash is deliberately introduced into synthetically dyed rugs to suggest age or a village feeling.

Misconception 6: New Oriental rugs are no longer made by hand. It always surprises me when someone who is prepared to buy an Oriental rug betrays that misconception. 'Handmade' is what Oriental rugs are all about. In fact, as I have said elsewhere in this book, when natural dyes and handspun wool are used, rugs today are made just as they were thousands of years ago.

Misconception 7: Oriental rugs are often made with child slave labor. This appalling condition (otherwise called bonded child labor) exists, but best estimates are that it takes place in only 1 to 3 percent of the workforce. Child labor that is not bonded is more common. The National Council for Applied Economic Research estimates that 8 percent of the workforce are children. That figure includes children who work at home on looms, attended by their parents. Conditions seem to be improving. Germany has been an especially effective force against illegal child labor, and recent U.S. legislation helps. Worldwide, the hand-knotted carpet industry has initiated programs that are promising. There is a trend among American producers to create schools for children. Rest assured that the producers whose stories you read in this book are among those who genuinely care about working conditions for children.

PART TWO

THE RUGS BY REGION

"Though Oriental rug making has always been responsive to Western markets, its essential spirit has remained grounded in the East. Now that Westerners control carpet production far more than ever, one wonders if that essential Eastern spirit is still intact, and what will happen if it's lost."

The following chapters are comprised of discussions and critiques of new Oriental rugs found in the market today, country by country. Stories of a few of the movers and shakers behind them are interspersed. These are interesting people and worth reading about for that reason. But beyond that, it's nice to know whose rug you are buying. I've found that good, solid people make good, solid rugs, and slippery folks make rugs you don't want to buy. Interestingly, though many of the 'movers and shakers' have launched large businesses, most seem to have been motivated less by money than by a desire to do it right. As one rugmaker (Dorje) from Nepal wrote, 'My mother is the main carpet guru for me and the background for all my work. She told me make the best and don't worry if you can't sell.' Two of the people I have written about gave up careers as attorneys and another a career as a psychologist to make rugs. Among the whole breed of manufacturers I talked with, only one is an MBA. They are or were poets, teachers, travelers, painters, and adventurers—and even the MBA is passionate about making rugs. Many of the pioneering rugmakers have names like Walter, Odegard, Sumner, and Robinson. It is hard to escape the conclusion that the renaissance in rugs is a Western-driven phenomenon—and indeed it largely is. But nearly every Westerner who has contributed to this phenomenal period of rugmaking has a counterpart in the East, a producer, partner, or trusted friend without whom they would likely not have succeeded. These folks from the East or Middle East are

Turkmen rug dealers and friends in Islamabad, Pakistan, 1989. (Chris Walter.)

under-represented here. I have written about them when I have had enough information, but often this is not available. Some of the producers back home are essentially trade secrets and their identity is kept obscure by their American clients, though a few American rugmakers have insisted that their producers be given proper credit.

As I have reviewed the production of rugs from each country, I believe I have discovered a phenomenon not previously noted: a fundamental change has occurred in the way rugs are selected to be woven. Weavers in thousands and thousands of villages across the Middle East and Asia have heretofore decided what rugs they would weave, and the market has been free to buy them or not. To be sure, some weavers have always made rugs under contract to merchants. Most large, carpet-sized rugs, for instance, are made this way: at the bidding of city merchants. Yet the production of most rugs was initiated by the weavers themselves. My sense is that this may no longer be true. Commercial interests in Europe and America are now deciding what carpets will be made. Certainly the greater part of the rugs imported into America (which, of course, do not include the carpets of Iran) are now made by weavers who are merely filling orders from American firms. Most are under contract to American importers who are making the decisions about what designs are to be woven, as well as what kind of dyes will be used, and so on.

There is cause to be concerned about this. Though Oriental rug making has always been responsive to Western markets, its essential spirit has remained grounded in the East. Now that Westerners control carpet production far more than ever, one wonders if that essential Eastern spirit is still intact, and what will happen if it's lost. Personally, though I am concerned, I find enough positive elements in the situation that I am optimistic. I believe that the involvement of Westerners since the late 1970s has been one of the greatest causes for the happy turnaround in the industry in Asia and the Middle East, and, indeed, in the art form as a whole. Perhaps, as James Opie suggested, the West is now making amends for past sins (such as introducing very poor quality synthetic dyes to the rug-

making East in the nineteenth century) by helping restore some of the rug-making techniques and designs lost to many of the weavers during the past sixty years. I recognize the controversial nature of what I am writing about here. First, there is not the right kind of data available for me to prove my assertion that rug production has been fundamentally changed in this regard; I base it on my subjective response to what I see in the market here and elsewhere. Second, I know that many who care about Oriental rugs will find nothing at all positive in the situation if I am right, and the West is now fundamentally calling the shots about what rugs are being made and how. The argument certainly won't be resolved here, but you may want to consider it as we survey those on the market today.

It has not been possible for me to speak here of every kind of new rug you will meet in the market. I have weighted the discussion toward those that contributed most to this period of renaissance. But please don't think that a rug is unworthy if you don't find it here. There are far more good rugs than it is possible to illustrate. On the other hand, I have illustrated a few not because they are the best, but because they are important rugs in the market and you will want to know about them.

The renaissance is not about natural dyes or handspun wool exclusively. It is not exclusively about a revival of antique designs or a creative new crop of contemporary designs. It is about all of these, and more: it is about the new cheap rugs in the market which are so much better than the former cheap rugs, about Arts and Crafts designs, and rugs designed from village life. It is about war rugs and soft-colored decorative rugs. It is about kilims. The renaissance in Oriental rugs is the sum total of everything good in the market. It is the astonishing wealth of choices we have today.

Chapter 4

The Rugs and Carpets of Turkey

Harald Böhmer, on far left, Bill McDonnell of Return to Tradition to his right, and DOBAG colleagues in Yuntdag region, Turkey, 1996.

The undisputed first mover of the renaissance of Oriental rugs was a German chemist named Harald Böhmer. In 1960 he took a seven-year teaching job in Turkey and, like many Westerners before and since, fell in love with Turkish rugs. He was different, though, in being especially interested in the dyes in Turkish rugs. When his teaching contract expired, he took the first opportunity to return, and in 1974 was again teaching in Turkey. In the meantime he had learned the language and had fallen in love with the country. His interest in rugs and dyes became a passion. When he learned of a method of analyzing dyes in fabrics (thin layer chromatography), he began an exhaustive, methodical analysis of dyes in Turkish rugs. Not only did he succeed in identifying the dyes used in hundreds of carpets of all ages, but he was able to decipher the actual processes involved in formulating the dyes and applying them to wool yarn. More to the point, he learned what natural dyestuffs rugmakers had used 100 years earlier, before the dyer's art had been lost, and in some cases he learned how these artisans had used them.

As Dr. Böhmer's second tenure as a teacher in Turkey was nearing an end, he conceived the notion of teaching Turkish rug weavers the art of dyeing with natural substances. Faced with the problem of making a living, he petitioned various German and Turkish institutions, and eventually the School of Fine Arts in Istanbul enthusiastically agreed to sponsor a project with Dr. Böhmer as chief advisor, called DOBAG—an acronym from Turkish words meaning Natural Dye Research and Development Project. An enriched weaving industry was envisioned which might keep country people at home rather than flooding the cities. An area in western Turkey was chosen: Ayvacik, full of small villages with long weaving traditions. By 1981 Dr. Böhmer was launched on his new career, and the world of Oriental rugs was about to change. Villagers eagerly learned to use natural dyes, and within a very short time were weaving rugs dyed from madder root, indigo, oak galls, and other vegetal materials, prepared, with a few improvements, just as the villagers' grandparents had prepared them.

As soon as the DOBAG project began to show some commercial success, weavers in the Ayvacik area who were not part of the DOBAG project began producing their own natural-dyed rugs, often copies of Caucasian rugs. Though Dr. Böhmer carefully controlled the quality of the DOBAG rugs and, in a broad sense, controlled the types of rugs made by DOBAG weavers, he had no control over the spin-offs. Thus these new natural-dyed rugs fared the way goods always do in a free market: under the control of no single person and free to blunder or thrive. Dr. Böhmer had created a benign monster over which, in the end, he had little control.

He and other principals did, though, control the DOBAG project, and the choices he made and the direction in which he pointed the project are interesting and controversial. The DOBAG rugs could have been anything: recreations of the earliest and best rugs in the history of rugmaking, of the earliest and best Turkish rugs, of the best rugs in the Ayvacik tradition—or they could have been rugs in designs entirely of the weavers' own choosing. Dr. Böhmer and his colleagues at DOBAG chose a conservative path: DOBAG rugs were to be in the Ayvacik tradition as it had evolved to that time and as the weavers found it in the early 1980s. The first designs were drafted for the weavers, but as soon as possible the drawings were done away with so that designs could evolve naturally. DOBAG was conscientious about not interfering with the villagers' traditional weavings. DOBAG can hardly be faulted for this sound and sensitive approach, but one has to realize that it left opportunities unexplored, in particular the opportunity to put the weavers back in touch with the masterpieces of their ancestors. After all, the Ayvacik tradition had suffered some of the same decline that nearly all other rugs had experienced during the preceding fifty years or so. The designs inherited by DOBAG weavers in 1982 simply were not as wonderful as their nineteenth-century antecedents—or so it seems to me.

A Turkish carpet from the DOBAG collective. Though only a small number of rugs are woven by DOBAG weavers larger than 6 by 9′, this 14 by 22-foot piece is certainly an exception. It was commissioned by the British Museum of London for use on the floor of one of its Islamic Arts rooms.

Azeri from Woven Legends. Weavers are given plenty of latitude to improvise in Azeris and, as a result, something of the weavers' personalities gets expressed. If it were not for that, this carpet, with all its straight lines, may well have come off feeling very stiff and rigid. It is about 9' by 12½', and a study in natural dyes.

I first heard word of DOBAG rugs from Ron O'Callahan, publisher of a new magazine at the time called *Oriental Rug Review*. The rugs turned out to be quite pleasing, with gorgeous, harmonious colors. They are tasteful and have likable, village designs. Their wool is first-rate, and the rugs have excellent body. They are certain to last for many decades and to age gracefully; they have the unmistakable stamp of quality. But I have personal reservations about them. They seem a bit stiff to me, not literally but figuratively. There seems little in them to capture the imagination except the story behind them, which, to be sure, is the best rug story in the world. Perhaps it is their lack of irregularity that I react badly to—which, I admit, sounds perverse. They have little abrash. They do not seem idiosyncratic to me or fanciful. Obviously, this is a matter of personal taste, and I will be delighted if you disagree. I may be prejudiced by DOBAG's policy of selling rugs only through stores created especially for them, an approach

unique in the business. Only in speaking with **Bill McDonnell** of **Return to Tradition**, one such store in San Francisco, have I come to appreciate the rationale for the decision. Still, I wonder whether DOBAG weavings may have lost a certain healthy pressure to evolve in not being offered shoulder to shoulder with rugs of other weavers and producers.

DOBAG was the start of the renaissance, but **George Jevremovic** (Yev REM o vich…but everyone in the industry refers to him as George) took it to the next level under the company name **Woven Legends**. In 1977 he left graduate school in the States, where he studied literature, history, and creative writing, and followed his girlfriend to Turkey. He took up permanent residence there beginning in 1979, at first teaching in an American school in Istanbul, then buying and selling old Turkish rugs and kilims. In 1980 he and his Turkish girlfriend, **Neslihan Christobel**

Jevremovic, were married. (Neslihan, an engineer, joined the family business in 1987 and has since been a 50 percent owner and an important part of the business. She and George work together amicably though they are no longer married.) George was in love with antique carpets, and bored by new rugs. The crucial difference, he came to believe, was that old rugs were made from natural dyes and new rugs from synthetic. But he was impressed when, in 1981, he first saw DOBAG-inspired rugs from the villages around Ayvacik. He proceeded to buy hundreds of small pieces, selling them to dealers in New York. In 1982 he opened his own wholesale business in Philadelphia. By the following year he was asking weavers around Ayvacik to make rugs in runner sizes for him, some of them in his own designs. But he began to realize that the tribal nature of Ayvacik culture constrained him from making the kinds of rugs that really interested him. He wanted to make large pieces, and that required an infrastructure he didn't think Ayvacik could support. He wanted the same kind of charm and naivete in large rugs that one usually finds only in small ones, and he wanted to weave rugs in early designs, especially designs from northern Iran.

During a several year period, from 1984 to 1987, George Jevremovic slowly established a production, first in Karaman in south central Turkey, then Erzerum in eastern Turkey, finally Malatya, also in the east. These were difficult years. All the money from the sale of old rugs went into starting up the new business. But the major obstacle was a lack of models for what he was trying to do. Everything had to be put in place. For advice on natural dyeing, he brought several enthusiasts from the U.S. Although handspun wool was still available in Turkey, quantities fell far short of what he needed. Eventually Woven Legends employed 15,000 people and sometimes more: spinners, weavers, dyers, and others. A lot of money was passing hands. Often George Jevremovic had no idea whether he would ever again see some of the people he was forced to advance money to. He was concerned about his inexperience in buying wool. He heard that wool, which is sold by the pound, could absorb up to one-third its weight in water without feeling wet. How much water was he buying with every pound of wool? He did find the occasional rock at the bottom of a bag of wool. Mr.

Jevremovic estimates that production was about 100 meters a month in 1984, 300 in 1985, and 1000 meters a month in 1986.

(In talking with George Jevremovic, I began to realize how much more difficult it is to produce large rugs (carpets) than small. 'The act of weaving a large rug,' he told me, 'requires a level of organization most rural areas can't handle.' One concept that startled me: when a large carpet is woven, the finished part is rolled around a drum, not to be seen again until the piece is finished and cut off the loom. A carpet may be on a loom for months and months. That is plenty of time to forget details of design and colors on the part that was long rolled up. You can see why things sometimes go wrong with, let's say, a 12 by 18-foot carpet. To me the miracle is how often they *don't*.)

It would be hard to exaggerate just how important Woven Legends has been in the rug industry since around 1985—which, not coincidentally, is when I believe the rug renaissance began. The DOBAG Project revived the use of natural dyes, but **Azeri** carpets (pronounced variously, but usually AH zer ee) which were the principal product of Woven Legends for a decade or more, took it to the next level. Though they were more expensive than all but a few other new rugs, Azeris demonstrated that relatively expensive natural-dyed carpets could still be commercially successful. Secondly, Woven Legends demonstrated that it was possible to make carpets—i.e. room-sized rugs—with a genuine village look. Up to that time, nearly every large rug, old or new, was curvilinear and formal looking. People who liked old tribal and village rugs were hard-pressed to find carpet-sized pieces they could live with before Azeris. Furthermore, Woven Legends showed that antique designs could be convincingly rendered in new carpets. Azeri designs were wonderful—mostly derived from northern Iran. In addition, they were the first new rugs with absolutely palpable character. This was due, in part, to another first in a major commercial production of new carpets: weavers were allowed the freedom to improvise—not unlimited freedom, but enough that weavers managed to imbue them with their individual spirit.

These lessons were not lost on other manufacturers. Many copied Azeris directly. Almost every rugmaker was

Azeri. It is almost the opposite of the Azeri above. Rather than being tribal in feeling, it is curvilinear and formal looking. Carpets with green fields were rare before the early 1990s.

Azeris are woven in hundreds of designs, but this may be the quintessential Azeri. It looks vaguely north Persian, south Persian, west Persian and Caucasian. It is tribal in feeling, but is nearly 9' by 12'. It has strong colors that, though saturated, still are not in the least garish. And it has a capricious quality that Azeris often have.

influenced. Eventually mail-order catalogues offered machine-made knockoffs!

(Azeri is a copyrighted trade name owned by Woven Legends. George Jevremovic, Woven Legends' founder, now regrets the choice of name. The word comes from a group of Turks who make rugs in Turkey and the Caucasus; Azerbaijan is named after them. Rugmakers looking to circumvent the copyright have been quick to exploit the difficulty inherent in trying to copyright the name of a people. Nearly fifteen years after the inception of the Azeri, it is still the most widely copied rug in Turkey, and dealers who sell copies often call them Azeris. In recent years, genuine Azeris have been labeled as such on the back of one corner.)

Today some of the thunder of Azeris has been stolen by the legions who jumped on the wagon and began copying them in Turkey and elsewhere, and for the past several years much of the decorative market has demanded softer colors than those found in Azeris. But Azeris have continued to evolve, changing not so much with the market as with the whimsy of their creator, George Jevremovic. In fact, 'whimsical' and 'playful' are good words to describe a side of Azeris that no manufacturer has managed to duplicate. We see Azeris whose designs consist of nothing but fish, others full of teacups, and one series shows people playing golf. Miraculously, they manage to look like Oriental rugs. The knot count of Azeris ranges from about 49 to 64 Turkish knots per square inch. They are on cotton foundations with a heavily depressed warp. Most have huge body: they are very heavy rugs. The majority sell for around $60 per square foot.

Another original product of Woven Legends is the line of rugs called **Folklife**. Weavers are encouraged to weave whatever they like, and most often they choose scenes from village life: children playing ball, livestock, houses, and so on. Nearly everyone is charmed by these rugs, though a customer of mine decided not to buy one she was considering when she discovered that the houses in the rug had television antennas. Like so many other rugs from Woven Legends, Folklife rugs have been copied by others, but the copies are never as good.

When I asked George Jevremovic which of all the new rugs he considered collectible, he apologized for being prejudiced, but said he liked 'some of the Turkish rugs'. What about them does he like? He cited their 'tension'. I asked him to explain. He said he admires the weavers in China and India who make rugs for him and partner Teddy Sumner's Black Mountain Looms. These weavers are agreeable and cooperative and skillful. He has a different experience when he asks Turkish weavers to weave rugs

To me, there is something jarring about the color of this Azeri's border in relation to its field. Is that its downfall, or its hook—the charming oddity that fascinates? It is about 10' by 12', and based on old north Persian Heriz district carpets.

A Folklife rug from Woven Legends. Weavers improvise whatever village scene they choose. This rug is about 6½′ by 9′.

from drawings. They too are skillful and would like to please. But there is just something in them—'DNA', he calls it—that makes them a little resistant to following someone else's drawings. 'The tension,' he says, 'is between their desire to break away and their desire to become part of the process. They fight the rapids.' That tension translates into something tantalizing in their rugs, something personal—something George Jevremovic responds to.

Another good Woven Legends product is known as **Yatak**. Yataks are heavy-bodied and coarsely knotted, inspired by simple Turkish village rugs and evidently by south Persian rugs called Gabbehs [gah BAY]. They are playful and charming, stuffed, as it were, with color and wool—the same natural dyes and good Turkish wool that are in Azeris. They are unpretentious, fun, spirited, and bargains: about $45 per square foot for rugs made with natural dyes and handspun Turkish wool!

A relatively new line of rugs from Woven Legends, evidently created in response to shifting market demand for lighter and softer colors, is called **Rubia**. Rubias have the same heavy body, natural dyes, and handspun wool as Azeris, but the colors are softer. Woven Legends also makes Fine Rubias, which are just what you expect: like Rubias, but finer, with about 90 knots per inch. A colleague, Paul Ramsey, believes that some fine Rubias are among the best carpets ever made.

There has been a price to pay for the freedom Woven Legends permits its weavers and the lack of control inherent in any production using natural dyes. The quality of carpets varies widely. Sometimes abrash is so pronounced as to be disturbing. Weaving can be uneven, edges may curl. Consequently, prices can vary greatly. Some retailers buy large quantities of the not-so-great pieces cheaply and sell them cheaply. Other dealers choose them as carefully as if they were valuable antiques (which, I am convinced, they someday will be) and charge more for them. Prices vary from $40 to $70 per square foot. Examine every Woven Legend rug carefully, and make certain that you are buying a real one. If you buy a good rug from Woven Legends, you will have bought the very best of what the rug renaissance has to offer.

As the decorative rug market began to demand a more refined look in the late '80s, George Jevremovic and **Teddy Sumner** of Michaelian and Kohlberg of New York formed a business in partnership called **Black Mountain Looms** and produced a new line of rugs and carpets called **Kentwilly**, named after their sons. Kentwillys are clipped shorter than Azeris and have 'flat backs' or no warp depression, rather like a Persian Mahal, so they feel less chunky and more blankety than Azeris. They are made in designs ranging from Arts and Crafts to old designs from the Arak or Sultanabad district of Iran.

One of the earliest and best productions from Turkey was created by a Turkish gentleman named **Suat Izmirili**, who established **Anadol Oriental Rugs** in 1984. He was joined about seven months later by **Paul McSweeny**, who has been an important part of the business since then. At first, Anadol produced rugs with synthetic dyes, convinced that natural dyes were not practical. But when Woven Legends' example proved them wrong, 'two weeks later we were using natural dyes,' says Paul McSweeny with characteristic good humor. Today Anadol makes among the best rugs in Turkey, all in natural dyes and handspun wool. But, faced with production problems there, Anadol has largely shifted its production to Egypt and Romania in a business called Antique Looms. (You can read more about Antique Looms in Chapter Eleven.)

Turkey was where the whole revolutionary pot started boiling: first the German project, DOBAG, then Woven Legends and all those influenced by Woven Legends, all of them experimenting with natural dyes and handspun wool. For perhaps eight years, Turkey was the only major source for the new breed of naturally dyed rugs. Now, at the end of the 1990s, the center for natural-dyed rugs has largely shifted to Pakistan and India. I was surprised, in surveying new Turkish rugs, to realize to what extent Turkey's present contribution to the market has fallen off. The greatest obstacle to making importable rugs in Turkey has been the rising cost of labor, especially weaving. That is why a number of manufacturers are now having Turkish wool dyed there and sending it to other countries for weaving. But beyond rising costs, manufacturers complain about a Turkish mind-set that results in inconsistent rugs. Paul McSweeny of Anadol says that, of ten rugs that

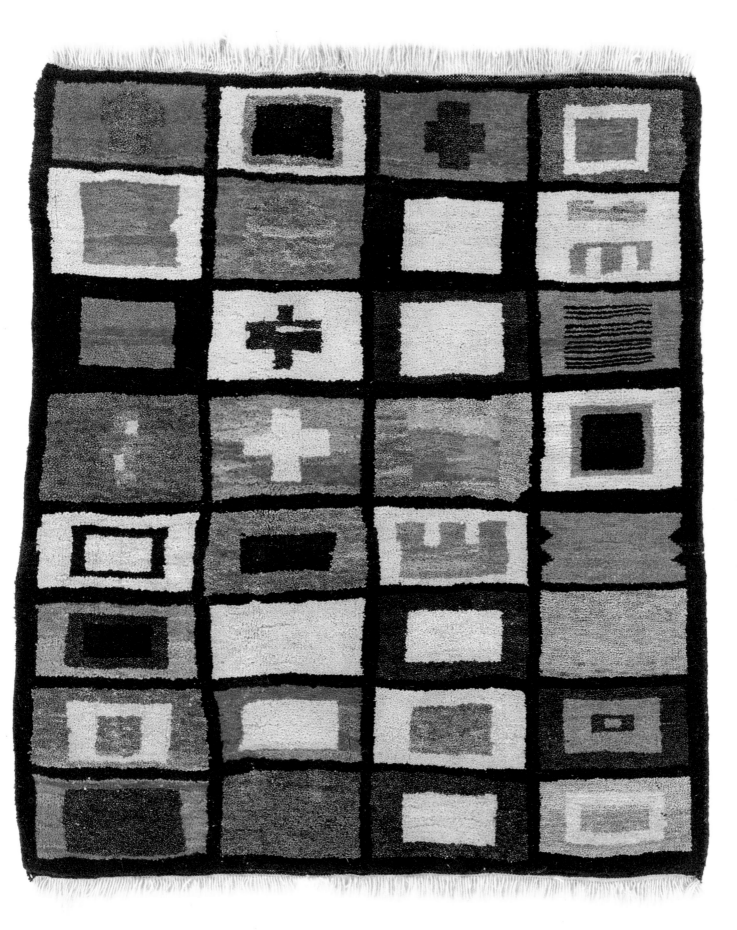

Yatak from Woven Legends. Less finely knotted than Azeris and clipped longer in pile, Yataks are the essence of tribal art.

A Rubia from Woven Legends. Most Rubias are a bit softer in color than Azeris, and perhaps they look a bit more refined. It is hard to say what inspired this carpet; most likely it was an old Mahal from Iran.

Rubia from Woven Legends. Woven Legends successfully manages to render very intricate, formal designs in a slightly loose or relaxed way. Like Persian Bijars, they often seem to have one foot in the city and the other in the countryside.

A Kentwilly from Black Mountain Looms. Most Kentwillys are made in Turkey, though some are woven in Romania with wool raised and dyed in Turkey. They are clipped shorter than Azeris, and tend to be a little more citified.

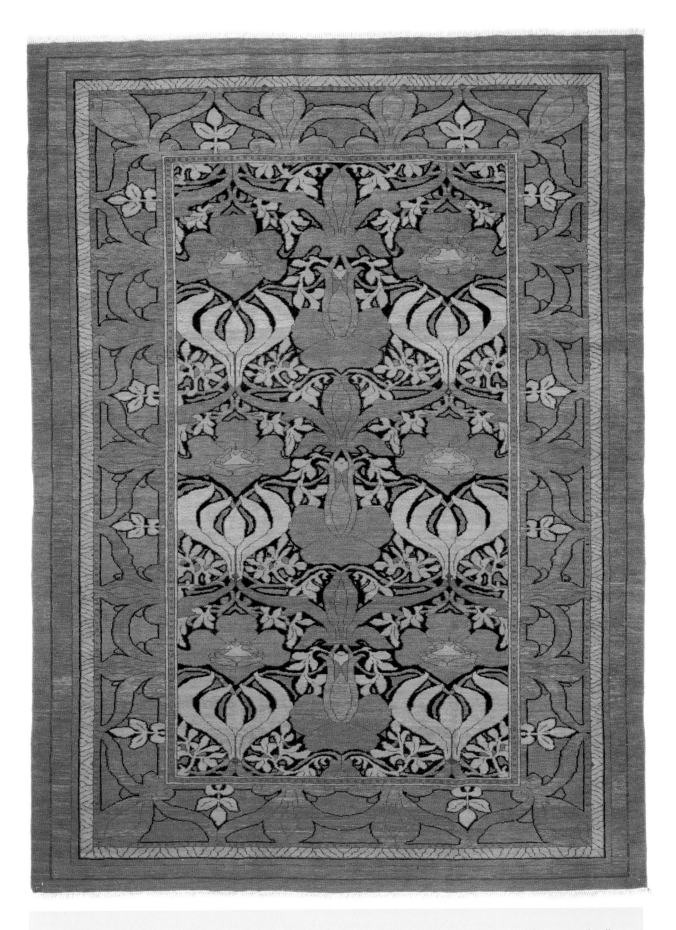

Kentwilly from Black Mountain Looms. This carpet was modeled after Arts and Crafts rugs from around the turn of the century. Like all Kentwillys, it was made with vegetal dyes and handspun wool.

A gorgeous Elvan from Anadol, made in Turkey. Use your magnifying glass to see the subtle camel-colored vining figures in the 'background' of the field. Natural dyes, handspun wool pile.

From Anadol Oriental Rugs. It appears to have been based on Persian Sultanabads which, at the beginning of the millenium, seem to be the most inspiring models for rug-makers. Anadol calls it an Elvan.

come off their looms, two will be blockbusters, four will be okay, and the last four perhaps not saleable. Izi Mizrahi of I. M. International, born in Turkey and a veteran rug-maker there, reports similar frustrations that have driven him to shift much of his production to Pakistan. It is no wonder that many producers have given up on Turkey. Still, there is the phenomenon of George Jevremovic's 'tension', the upshot of which is that the few blockbuster pieces that come off Turkish looms are so good that they make all the grief worthwhile—if, as a consumer, you can get your hands on them.

Turkish Kilims still pour out of Turkey. Most are inexpensive, usually 3 by 5 or 4 by 6 feet with pleasing colors, though synthetically dyed. Typically they are made in a slit-tapestry weave, on wool warps, and sell for $325 to $550 each. From time to time we see fantastic new kilims from Turkey that are breathtakingly fine and beautiful and are made with natural dyes. Turkish pieces as finely woven as these have been unknown in the market until recently.

Synthetic dyed rugs from western Turkey continue to be available, especially from **Yagcibedir** (YAJ e be dir) and **Dosmealtu** (Dosh mee AL tu). They are disappointing rugs, though, to those of us who have seen their charming, natural-dyed ancestors. Essentially they have two colors, red and blue.

American tourists still return from Turkey with **Kaiseri** rugs made in central Anatolia. Local rug merchants represent them as silk rugs. In fact, they are made with mercerized cotton, a poor imitation. I have examined pile fibers from many Kaiseris in microscopes without finding one that is really silk. Those who have purchased 'silk' Kaiseris in Turkey, still in denial after hearing the bad news, sometimes produce receipts from Turkey that read, 'Made from 100% pure art silk.' Art silk? 'Art' turns out to be an abbreviation for 'artificial', without the period. That

is a refinement of the older version: 20 years ago, Kaiseri dealers told people they were made from 'Turkish silk', a euphemism for cotton. Before that, it was called 'German silk'. Having noted that, I must add that I have seen Kaiseris I like, cotton pile notwithstanding. Kaiseri weavers also make rugs with wool pile on a cotton foundation, though they are rarely imported into the U.S.

Though not often seen in the American market, the **silk Hereke** (HAIR eh keh) is still woven in Turkey. They are scarce here because few will pay the price for these amazingly fine rugs: $300–500 per square foot for ordinary pieces (which are quite fine) and, it is said, as much as $50,000 per square foot for pieces with 3000 to 4000 knots per square inch! Herekes are made in northwestern Anatolia near Istanbul, where production dates back to at least the middle of the nineteenth century. Lavish rugs were produced there in court workshops, and lavish rugs are made there still. Elsewhere I have cautioned that Chinese and even Egyptian silk rugs are sometimes imported into Turkey and sold as Herekes, but I am hard pressed to tell you how you can be certain that you are buying a real one. I have read that all Herekes are Persian-knotted, and I have read that all but a very few are Turkish-knotted. The confusion is understandable: one must be blessed with extraordinary vision to even *see* knots this small. In my experience, most new Herekes are Turkish-knotted, and you can rest assured that a very fine, new, silk rug that is Turkish-knotted is neither a Chinese nor an Egyptian copy, since both these are Persian-knotted. It is said that inscriptions are woven into Herekes to identify them, but there are exceptions. Some Herekes are both very fine and uninscribed, so an inscription or the lack of one is not a reliable guide to authenticity.

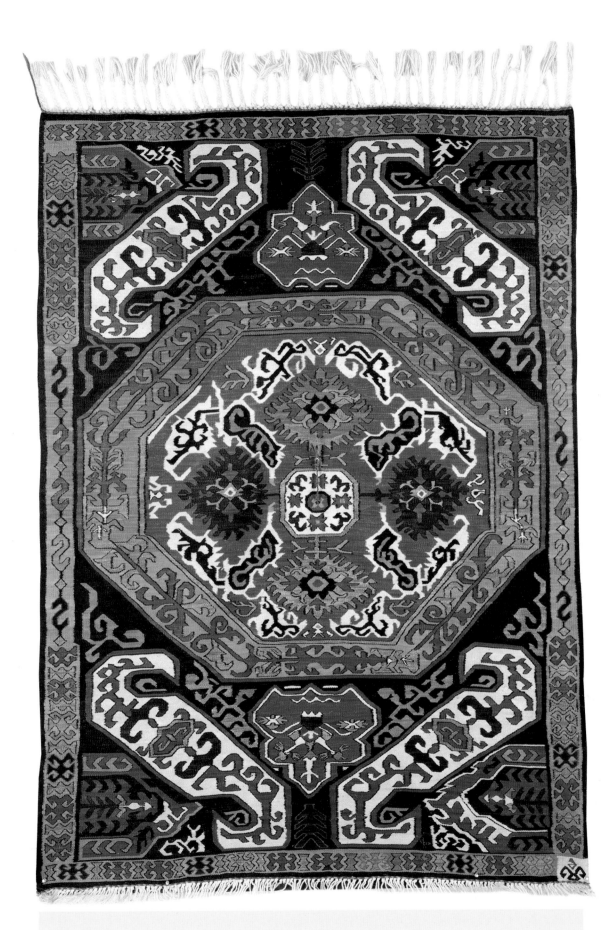

Turkish kilim from Konia. This is a marvelous piece with natural dyes and handspun wool. It was modeled after an exceptionally good Caucasian embroidery. Imported by Paul Ramsey of Denver. (David Holbrook Young.)

Hereke also produces wool rugs on cotton foundations that are not nearly as fine as the silk pieces. For a time in the 1980s wool-piled Herekes were often seen in the market, and they were quite good. But weavers near Hereke noted the success of these rugs and began to copy them, weaving rugs of inferior quality for a bit less money, and selling them as Herekes. The result was that Hereke's reputation was hurt and its industry suffered—a pattern repeated all too often in the rug world.

Silk Hereke from Turkey. This fantastic little rug is only one by one and a half feet, but it contains over 260,000 hand-tied knots (more than 1200 per square inch). Courtesy of Rumiko Ikeda.

Chapter 5

**The Rugs and Carpets
Of Tibet and Nepal**

In 1949 the Chinese invaded Tibet, and inadvertently changed the modern history of Oriental carpets. Before then, Tibetans made rugs for their own uses, which often involved religious ceremonies. There was little, if any, commerce in new Tibetan rugs outside Tibet (though today the oldest rugs from Tibet are among the most desirable to collectors). The Chinese invasion forced thousands of Tibetans to flee, and many who survived the journey out of the mountains took weaving skills with them to Nepal and India, where they established carpet industries to support themselves. In Nepal, no carpet industry had existed before the Tibetan refugees created one.

Today, Tibetan rugs (by which name all rugs made by Tibetans are known, whether woven in Nepal, Tibet, or India) are among the brightest stars in the rug firmament. A retailer in Reno, Nevada tells me that 60 percent of all his sales are in Tibetan rugs. Twenty-five years ago, during the formative stages of the Tibetan rug industry, things could not have been more different. Most of the Tibetan rugs reaching the United States were made with luster-less, machine-spun Indian wool in bright synthetic dyes. Sizes were limited and designs were interesting only in their novelty.

Behind the scenes, though, a family of Tibetan rug dealers in Katmandu, Nepal was quietly learning the moribund art of dyeing with natural plant dyes. These are the words of a Tibetan refugee named Dorje written in August of 1998 and faxed to Stephanie Odegard: 'Early '70s during my school vacation, I used to be at our shop Lhasa Curio Shop in Jochen tole, probably the first Tibetan antique shop that time. I found lots of people asking me about the dyes on the old carpets with veg-dyes. It interest me to inquire and learn too. I have been asking many older Tibetans and finally in 1977 we had invited two old women teaching us the indigo dyes in Tibetan methods. I learnt indigo dyeing with this women and others I learnt through Tibetan medical institute when my cousin sister and her husband were student in the institute. Vegetal dyeing they found in Medicinal Buddha textbook. They gave me the theory and I experimented myself and learnt them. In 1975 I started working for Tamdi and Sons…I think Thombo and Tent Tom were working in carpets around the same time… Natural and vegetal dyeing is very old

tradition of this world. The only thing exception is the different recipe of one person to another person. It is like wine making or even cooking.'

Later, Dorje became Stephanie Odegard's producer. Dorje's brother Tsetan became James Tufenkian's producer, and Namgyl, who was 'one of [Dorje's] staffs for a few years' became Steve Laska's producer. But I have gotten ahead of my story.

In 1975, the rugs reaching the American market from Nepal were poor things with bright synthetic dyes and Indian wool; but there were a few Tibetans like Dorje who retained knowledge of the old ways of making rugs. This is what Americans and Europeans encountered as they began to explore the possibilities in Katmandu in the 1970s. One of them was called Tombo, a young American who has become a semi-mythical figure to the expatriates who knew him and those who have merely heard stories about him. In the mid to late 1970s, at the same time that Harald Böhmer, later of the DOBAG Project, was researching natural dyes in Turkish rugs, Tombo (Thomas Guta) was weaving rugs in Katmandu with natural dyes he had mixed himself. Almost certainly he had been taught by Tsetan or Namgyl, who in the '70s ran a shop called Vegetable Dyed Carpets. Inexplicably, Tombo was able to achieve rich, saturated colors with natural dyes more than a decade before that feat was duplicated by other Westerners. I met Tombo and saw his rugs sometime in the early 1980s when he visited my shop in Berkeley. My memory of the meeting is hazy, except that he seemed quite intense. But I remember his rugs. I admired them, but recall suggesting that he was asking too much for them. I wish I had bought at least one and kept it; I believe his may be the first natural-dyed rugs woven by any Westerner. Along with Dorje, Tsetan and Namgyl, he influenced a number of Westerners living in Nepal at the time, who were soon experimenting with rugs made in natural dyes. Dorje writes of Tombo: 'Thombo is what people used to call for Thomas Gutta who died several years ago in the plane accident in Katmandu. I heard Thombo had a Japanese wife and they did fine silk brocade weaving. I think his whole family died in that plane accident.'

For some years, a small number of Westerners made rugs in Nepal with natural dyes and imported them into

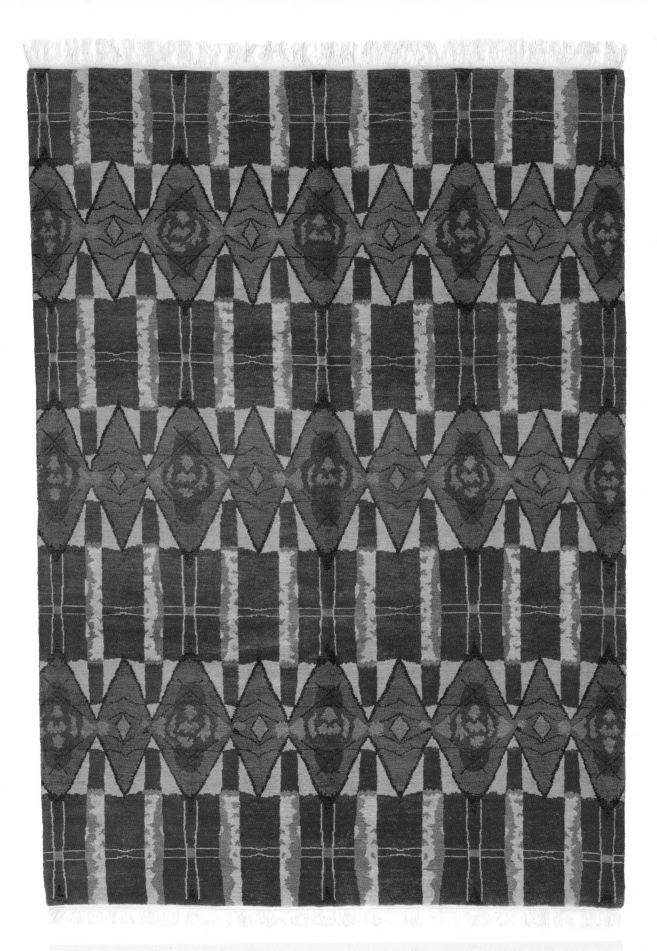

A Tibetan rug by Endless Knot of Petaluma, California. The rug is made with chrome dyes, handspun wool pile, and an excellent finish. As far as I am concerned, it is a work of art.

Germany and America. But in the end, natural dyeing barely managed to survive, kept alive by just one or two Americans (including Stephanie Odegard) and a few Tibetan refugees. German importers had long been interested in Tibetan carpets, but quantities available in the market were limited by a lack of wool. Wool was scarce to begin with, but the greatest impediment to obtaining adequate supplies was corruption among the government officials who regulated it. Working through the World Bank for which she was a consultant, Stephanie Odegard helped apply pressure that finally allowed wool to flow freely into the market. The logjam created by the lack of wool was finally broken in 1987, and by 1989 a kind of stampede was under way. Germans in particular were in a buying frenzy (Nepalese rug people joked that Germans ate Tibetan rugs for breakfast), and rugmakers in Nepal geared up to supply them. The majority of German buyers are not known to be choosy, and no effort was made to supply them with natural-dyed carpets. In fact, German buyers generally do not like the irregularities that natural dyeing entails. So the natural dye movement in Nepal stalled around 1987, de-selected by market conditions.

One of the early producers of rugs in Nepal was **Steve Laska** from Northern California. He went to Nepal in 1977 with an antecedent interest in natural-dyed rugs, stimulated by an earlier adventure importing Mexican Indian rugs to the U.S. He lived in Nepal from 1977 through 1979 and was aware of Tombo's rugs, all of which were in traditional Tibetan designs. Mr. Laska's particular vision was that there was no reason to restrict designs in Tibetan rugs to traditional Tibetan motifs. Any design at all (except the finest) could be woven in Tibetan rugs. But, strapped for money, he simply didn't have the resources to launch anything but a tiny production of natural-dyed carpets even as he watched other Americans become big players. By the mid-'80s, Steve Laska was designing his own rugs and selling them in the San Francisco Bay Area. Eventually he named his business **Endless Knot Rug Company**, which he ran part time at first while earning a Masters degree in psychology. Eventually he gave up his practice as a clinical psychologist to concentrate on making rugs.

Over the years, Endless Knot has continually moved forward with new and better designs in a huge range of colors (about 160 currently). Endless Knot rugs strike me as

having good staying power, not soon to become unfashionable as styles change. They are priced moderately: 60-knot rugs (that is, about 60 knots per square inch) usually cost less than $50 per square foot. Today Mr. Laska's contemporary designs are among the best around. Incredibly, Endless Knot is able to make *custom* rugs within three months and often less. I believe this to be a record in the industry.

From the outset, the modern Tibetan rug industry has been geared to the decorative rug market. It differs in that respect from the productions of other countries. The company most successful at capturing a national reputation in the decorative rug market is **Tufenkian Tibetan Carpets**, established by **James Tufenkian** (Tu FEN kee en). As a young man, James Tufenkian graduated from law school and moved directly into the Oriental rug business. Though based in New York, he paid his dues like many another small importer at the start of their career by motoring rugs to distant parts of the country to sell. More than once I bought rugs from James Tufenkian in Berkeley directly out of the trunk of his rented car. At first, beginning about 1982, he imported Afghan and Turkish goods, attracted by their tribal character. At that time most other Oriental rugs, though made by hand, lacked personality and may as well have been made by machines. After several years of importing and wholesaling, he experienced one of those moments that change people's lives. He bought a group of fine Turkmen rugs which he was very enthusiastic about, sold them all in two or three days, and was left to contemplate the fact that he could not replace them. It became clear to him that he had to manufacture rugs himself, so he headed to Nepal in about 1984 to get something going.

At the time that James Tufenkian began to manufacture them, Tibetan rugs were considered a risky specialty item, but probably more than any other single person he succeeded in making them leaders in the decorative rug market. He worked hard, told me once during those early days that he would retire in four years, and still is working hard fourteen years later. His are probably the only Tibetan rugs in the market that a sizable number of customers ask for by name. All but a very few Tufenkian rugs are made with handspun wool, which is standard in the best Tibetan rugs (though still rare elsewhere). In addition, Tufenkian

A rug by Tufenkian Tibetan Carpets, called Agra Border, palamino. Its wool pile was carded and spun by hand and colored with modern chrome dyes.

'Brisas, vineyard', is the name of this piece from Tufenkian. Of all rugmakers, those making Tibetan rugs seem most likely to feature contemporary design.

rugs are often made with wool that has been carded by hand. Carding is the process of untangling the wool fibers, essentially by combing them, before spinning them into yarn. Carding is almost always by machine now; Tufenkian's decision to continue with hand-carding adds to his rugs' handcrafted look. In addition, they all have excellent wool and good chrome dyes. They clearly take aim at the decorative rug market. Prices range from about $70 a foot for nominal 60-knot rugs to as much as $120 per foot for 100-knot pieces. (A 'nominal' knot-count means that the actual one is likely to be 10 percent less.)

> Tibetan rugs are unique. They have their own weave, their own materials, their own look, their own rules. My wife, Natasha, and I have commissioned several rugs to be made in Nepal and have learned to our grief that designs and colors that look good produced in, say, Turkey, look ridiculous in a Tibetan rug. Those who are successful at manufacturing Tibetan rugs have an admirable understanding of their medium. Most often Tibetan rugs have soft colors, spare designs, and a thick wool pile of Nepalese, Tibetan, or Chinese wool, sometimes mixed with Merino wool from Australia. In fact, it might be said that the essence of modern Tibetan rugs is their wool. The standard weave is a nominal 60 knots per inch, but weavers sometimes produce rugs with 80 and 100 knots. Like some Chinese rugs, most Tibetan ones have carved or sculpted pile. After a rug comes off the loom, specialists carve away some of the pile in lines, perhaps an eighth-of-an-inch deep, outlining elements of the design, and demarcating borders from fields. Perhaps you can picture the effect better by imagining a design carved into a flat piece of wood.

Of all the major importers of Tibetan rugs, Stephanie Odegard may have the deepest personal roots in Nepal and Tibet. She lived in Nepal in 1985 and 1986 while she worked as a consultant to the World Bank, helping to promote business in Nepal. During this time she began to produce rugs herself. It is interesting how influential she was in the carpet industry before she had made a single rug. Besides helping to open up the supply of wool in Nepal in her capacity as consultant to the World Monetary Fund, she helped sponsor workshops in natural dyeing in Nepal in 1985. During her time there, she was deeply engaged in collecting textiles, including old Tibetan rugs, and they

came to inspire the designs of her own Tibetan rugs. At first, Ms. Odegard tried to interest Stark, the prestigious East Coast retailer of fashionable carpets, in her product but, as she says, 'They didn't believe in them.' For several years, Teddy Sumner of Michaelian and Kohlberg imported and marketed Stephanie Odegard's rugs and carpets before she established her own wholesale business. Ms. Odegard's production has received extraordinary acclaim. In 1998 she was commissioned to create eight carpets for the new paintings galleries at the J. Paul Getty Museum in Southern California, and The Art Institute of Chicago licensed her to produce an entire line of rugs based on its collection of seventeenth-century textile fragments. The Odegard carpets at the Getty Museum are in natural dyes, as are many of the rugs she makes. Ms. Odegard may be the only person who has continued to use natural dyes in many of her rugs after the Germans' strong entry into the market in 1987. Odegard rugs always look like Odegard rugs, even though their designs vary greatly. Her signature rugs are simple one-and-two-color pieces that emanate a kind of quiet dignity and comfort. Prices range from about $60 per square foot for 60-knot rugs to $100 or more per square foot for 100-knot, vegetable-dyed rugs.

Teddy Sumner of **Michaelian and Kohlberg** in New York is one of the pioneers of the rug renaissance. (You can read more about him and his participation in Black Mountain Looms in Chapters Eight and Ten.) When he joined the family business (founded in 1921 by grandfather Frank Michaelian) in 1982, he quickly took it in unexpected directions—specifically, northeast to Nepal. By 1985, just as the rug renaissance was beginning to be felt, Teddy Sumner began importing Tibetan rugs, Stephanie Odegard's designs at first, then Mr. Sumner's own. They were in marked contrast to the simple, open-field Tibetan rugs that were made for the German market. Still in production today, they draw on many prototypes, including modern art, Arts and Crafts design, European textile design, traditional Tibetan motifs, and many others. They are lavishly textured rugs with wonderful wool, and, though they are made with chrome dyes, their wool pile is spun by hand. Prices are good: from about $53 a foot for 60-knot rugs to about $80 for 100-knot rugs.

A New York company named **Inner Asia Trading Company** produces an excellent line of Tibetan rugs called **Ganchen**. They are the only rugs made in Tibet by Tibetan weavers in Tibetan designs. The wool they are made of, called 'champhel' (Tibetan wool from the northern highlands), feels wonderful and is among the best in the world. The sheep that contribute their coats to the production of Ganchen rugs are raised at altitudes of up to 15,000 feet. Wool grown at those frigid heights develops very long strands and is rich in natural oils, making it lustrous and resilient. Most of Inner Asia's production is in 80 knots and made with hand-carded and handspun wool. One line, called **Folk Arts**, is made with natural dyes on a wool foundation, but Ganchens are made from chrome dyes on cotton foundations.

Chris Walter (about whom there is much more information in Chapter Six) founded the **Tibetan Natural Dye Weaving Project** in Nepal in 1990. Formed largely for the benefit of Tibetan refugees, the Project makes only natural-dyed rugs and carpets. Mr. Walter was familiar with the Nepalese natural dye rugs from the early 1980s. But he found their dyes lacking in saturation. (I can attest that at least some of those early natural-dyed rugs looked great but were unable to withstand even indirect sunlight. My wife and I bought a very pretty 6 by 9 rug that today is well loved but hopelessly faded.) Chris Walter's goal was to produce saturated colors in genuine Tibetan designs. As a result, the Tibetan Natural Dye Weaving Project rugs look very different from all other rugs made in Nepal. They have no 'decorator' look at all. Rather, they are like what old, unwashed, pre-synthetic Tibetan rugs must have looked like when new. Mr. Walter makes no effort to make them look old. Their prices are startlingly low: natural-dyed 60-knot rugs for about $40 per square foot.

Very recently I saw a groundbreaking Tibetan 100-knot rug made by a company called **Noreen Seabrook Marketing, Inc.**, run by longtime rug guru **Mike Marcy**. Inspired to make something that hadn't been made before, Mr. Marcy conceived the idea of simply not clipping the pile of a Tibetan rug that is otherwise manufactured the standard way. Let me explain: Unlike other rugs, the knots in Tibetan rugs are normally tied over a wooden rod. When the row of knots is completed, the rod is slipped out and the pile is clipped. Mike Marcy simply instructed his producer not to clip the pile in the final stage, leaving it, instead, looped and

looking a bit like the pile in Berber carpeting. In most of the rugs he makes, some of the pile is clipped and some is not, a mixture of techniques that he calls 'cut and loop'. The effect is very pleasing. Noreen Seabrook has developed the idea since its inception in 1994, and now offers rugs with this finish in seventeen different qualities. Average price for 100-knot cut and loop rugs is about $80 per square foot. With simple designs and light colors, these rugs are understated and very decorative.

A Tibetan rug by Odegard, Inc., in a Youngtse quality, called Pema Tsetan. Most of Stephanie Odegard's rugs and carpets are in the 100-knot weave, which is much finer than the more common 60-knot construction. Under incandescent light at night, this particular rug has a gorgeous, velvety glow. It is about 7' by 9'.

An Odegard Tibetan rug called Thicket. Though the two rugs illustrated here are quite elaborate, Ms. Odegard's signature look is almost the opposite: most are simple and understated.

This piece delights me. I feel I have come across a picture of its prototype in an auction catalogue sometime, someplace, and I believe that in its previous embodiment it was a textile. Now it is a Tibetan carpet from Michalean and Kohlberg in a 100-knot weave, about 7' by 11'. (Don Tuttle.)

Tibetan carpet from Michaelian and Kohlberg in a design called pomegranate. It is evidently a detail of an Arts and Crafts design (compare p. 137). The rug is manufactured in many different sizes.

A Ganchen from Inner Asia Trading Company, called Chrysanthemum and Vines, in a charcoal background. Inner Asia Trading Company is owned by a Tibetan and is the only company making rugs in Tibet by Tibetan weavers in Tibetan designs.

A rug from the Tibetan Natural Dye Weaving Project. All are in old Tibetan designs and are made with natural dyes. The project is largely for the benefit of Tibetan refugees in Nepal. (David Holbrook Young.)

You may have to look very closely at this rug to perceive that the white squares in the rug's center consist of unclipped pile. All the other areas have been clipped normally. The technique was developed and the rug made by Noreen Seabrook Marketing, Inc. of New York. The rug is about 4 by 5'. (David Holbrook Young.)

Chapter 6

The Rugs and Carpets of Pakistan

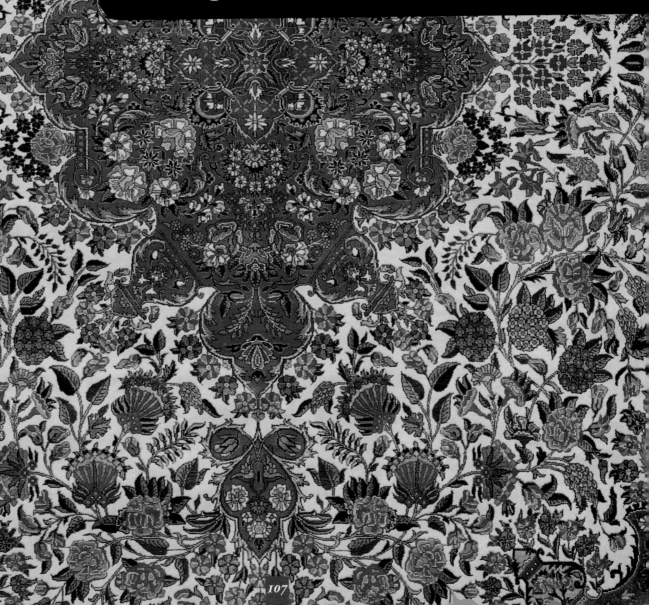

A Pakistani Bokhara, though not the most common kind. This piece, characterized by the two-panel field and what appear to be (but are not) prayer niches at one end of the rug, is known as a hachlu. It is about 3 by 5'. (David Holbrook Young.)

In 1977, a rug dealer and writer named Georges Izmidlian wrote: 'In countries where an informed body of opinion has grown up on the subject of oriental rugs, a distinction is drawn between those from Persia, Turkey, Afghanistan and Russia, and those from other areas which produce similar goods. Only the former are entitled to be described as real oriental rugs.' You will notice that that leaves out the rugs of Pakistan and India. It was rather harsh, even then—not even to consider Pakistani and Indian rugs 'real Orientals'—but at the time I might have agreed with him. Many still do. Pakistan was known for one kind of rug, the Pakistani Bokhara, produced by the thousands and sneered at as much for its popular success as for its aesthetic shortcomings. Pakistani Bokharas seemed especially vapid to a generation newly in love with tribal rugs. Further, it was thought that Pakistan had no tradition of rugmaking (no one has ever heard of an antique Pakistani rug, after all!), and that rug weaving in Pakistan was strictly commercial. Hence, Pakistani rugs were unreal.

Twenty-some years later, Pakistan and India arguably have contributed more to the rug revolution than any country except Turkey. A few people have even realized that if no one has ever heard of an antique Pakistani rug, it may be because Pakistan didn't exist until after WWII. Until then it was part of India. Some of history's greatest carpets were woven in Lahore, produced for the Mughal court in the seventeenth and eighteenth centuries. Indeed, Pakistan does have a rug tradition, quite a proud one. But old attitudes die hard, and most people whose knowledge about Oriental rugs was gained some years ago remain leery of Pakistani and Indian products. The truth today is that Pakistan's and India's best rugs are as good as rugs made anywhere (and just as expensive).

Pakistani Bokharas predate the rug renaissance, and though they are scorned by collectors, they have turned out to be honest rugs. Most are based on Turkmen prototypes called Tekkes, with repeating octagonal figures called guls, usually on fields of burgundy red, gray blue, or sometimes green. One line of these rugs is thick and of average weave, and they are known as 9/16 doubles, meaning that they have 144 knots per square inch. They are quite inexpensive (around $26 per square foot) and luxurious feeling because of their thick, soft wool, imported from either Australia or New Zealand. The standard

Bokhara, known in the trade as 10/20, is woven with a nominal 200 knots per square inch. A less often seen grade is known as 11/22 and has 242 knots per inch. This grade costs more, but I recommend paying the difference and buying it. A variant of the Tekke gul Bokharas is the **Hachlu**, usually available only in a 10/20 weave. These rugs are based on a Turkmen rug known as an 'engsi', and are recognizable by what appears to be (but is not) a series of prayer niches along one end and a field that is divided into quarters.

In the late 1970s, Pakistani rugmakers came up with a new product, known in the trade as the **Pakistani Persian** or the **Pakistani 16/18**, which is still made. As the second name implies, the knot-count of these rugs is a nominal 16 by 18 per square inch, for a total of 288. That is really quite a finely knotted rug, and the production has enjoyed deserved success. Designs almost always are Persian, the pile is Australian or New Zealand wool, body is very heavy, colors, though synthetic, are well chosen and attractive. They are sold in three grades called A, B, and C.

> It interests me that three different weavers, all working with the same number of knots per square inch, and all weaving the same design, produce rugs that differ radically in quality. Grade A Pakistani Persians are impressively clear on their surfaces. Details are discernible, designs are coherent. Grade C rugs, with the same number of knots per inch, seem out of focus, muddy, confused. What accounts for the difference? The weaver's skill. The rugs are graded upon completion, and weavers are paid on that basis.

Most likely, Pakistani Persian rugs were produced to fill the vacuum created when the U.S. ceased trading with Iran. At a time when U.S. dealers were no longer able to buy Persian rugs, Pakistani Persians were practically the only finely knotted, Persian-looking rugs available. Upon their introduction, square-foot prices were rather high: $75 a foot. Now they often sell for a bit less—around $65 per square foot.

The path for the rug renaissance in Pakistan was paved by Afghanistan's tragic civil war and the subsequent flood of Afghan refugees into neighboring Pakistan. More than a million Afghans sought refuge there, and, as the millenium nears, most still live in immigrant camps in Peshawar and

A Pakistani 'Persian', meaning a Pakistani rug in a Persian style. In the trade these are known as Pakistani 16/18s. Multiply those figures for the knots per square inch: 288. It was imported by Jerry H. Aziz, Inc. of New York. Though this piece is about 4' by 6', it is available 'in continuity', i.e. in all sizes.

Afghan refugees. They are spectators at a Buz Kashi match in Khorassan Camp near Peshawar, 1991. (Chris Walter.)

elsewhere near the Afghan–Pakistan border. Great numbers live in tents pitched in the desert. They segregate themselves by tribal alliances and language groups: Baluchis, Turkmen, Hazaras, and others. Among the immigrants are weavers who must number in the hundreds of thousands. Disrupted, cut off from their traditional means of making a living, they have perforce become receptive to new ideas and new designs. Westerners and others who would like rugs made to their specification approach producers with their requests. A contract is made between them, and the producer sees the project through to completion. Typically the producer creates graph paper drawings of designs, and supplies them to weavers along with dyed wool. Weavers work at their own looms or on looms owned by the producer. The system is flexible, quick, and readily available to anyone wanting rugs made to order. It largely accounts for the immense variety of rugs that make their way to the market.

Other Westerners take a far greater part in the rugmaking process. They become their own producers, supplying their own designs and materials and making scores of decisions about production details such as dyeing,

clipping, the color of the foundation material, finishing, and so forth. These people are the true rugmakers. One of the earliest and possibly still the largest is an American named **Chris Walter**, who has quietly created one of the very best and largest productions of natural-dyed rugs in the world in three separate businesses. Mr. Walter is a thoughtful listener, a soft-spoken, serious man, not given to self-promotion. Now in his 40s, he seems most comfortable sitting Eastern style on a carpet with Tibetan or Turkmen friends around a meal of pilaf, lentils, nann, and slices of fruit, speaking Tibetan or Turkmen or, for the sake of Western guests, a pidgin English. As a young man, he traveled in Turkey for two or three years, then attended and graduated from the University of Massachusetts in 1980 with a degree in anthropology. After school, he returned to Turkey, learned Turkish, and scoured remote villages for rugs, kilims, and trappings, then sold what he had unearthed in the United States. As it happened, he was on hand in Turkey exactly when DOBAG was born, and he watched as other natural dye projects spun off and began to flourish in the area of Ayvacik, then in Konia. That was in 1982 and '83. By 1986 Chris Walter was spending most of his time in East

Chris Walter and friends in Haripur Refugee Camp, 1989.

Turkestan and Pakistan where he made friends with Turkmen refugees from Afghanistan. He could communicate well with them, first through Turkish and then in their own dialect. He had begun to see that it would not always be possible to buy old pieces in Asia, and it occurred to him that he could make vegetal-dyed rugs in Pakistan based on what he had seen in Turkey. A Turkmen friend, Jora Agha, agreed, and with a small amount of money granted by a Cambridge-based organization called Cultural Survival, together they began to make Ersari rugs with handspun wool and natural dyes in an enterprise called the **Ersari Turkmen Cultural Project**. The weavers are Ersari refugees from Afghanistan, and the project was created largely for their benefit. Just as Harald Böhmer had done in Turkey, Chris Walter and Jora Agha decided to limit designs to those indigenous to the weavers, in this case the Ersaris (one branch of the Turkmen people). But unlike Dr. Böhmer, they felt free

to choose from the whole portfolio of Ersari weavings for designs, including some not woven in the last 100 years. For the next seven years they quietly experimented, improved, and perfected. No one else was doing anything similar in Pakistan, and they were left alone to work things out without competitive pressure. Even their awkward early products were well received in the United States because they were unique and captured the imagination. Some years later, Chris Walter and Jora Agha were able to establish two schools for the Ersaris. The schools are now teaching over 500 boys and girls with tuition fully paid by the Ersari weaving project.

Ersari weavers of the Weaving Project make rugs with traditional vegetal dyes, and I believe that, except for Mason Purcell's weavers, they are the only Turkmen people weaving rugs in Ersari designs with natural dyes. Certainly they are among the best Turkmen rugs in the world at the present. Designs are from the best Turkmen rugs made during the past 150 years. Their body is excellent, wool is lively, finishing first-rate. Above all, the Ersaris have somehow managed to capture the exact shade of red that makes antique Ersaris irresistible. These are pretty rugs, enjoyable, often signed by the weavers. Prices are good: around $45 per square foot. I recommend them highly.

Chris Walter speaks so matter-of-factly about creating industries and schools for refugees in Pakistan, about developing something like *four hundred* different designs among three projects, and about selling the rugs in the States and in Europe, that one loses sight of how difficult all this must have been. Anyway, in 1990 he began a new production in Pakistan with a Turkmen named Habibullah. The company was called **Yayla Tribal and Village Rugs**. Yayla (pronounced Yĭlah, with the accent on the first syllable) is the Turkmen word for the high summer pastures of nomadic shepherds. Chris Walter called the rugs they produced Aryana—the old name for northern Afghanistan, the Turkmen homeland. By the time he and Habibullah began the business, Mr. Walter already considered himself fortunate to have done so well with the Ersari project. Founding a large enterprise was not on his mind; instead, he was interested in producing rugs in natural dyes that he loved but could not make under the constraints of the Tibetan and Ersari projects. He certainly accomplished that, but inadvertently also launched what turned out to be a good-sized, important enterprise.

Under the direction of Habibullah and his family (who were originally from Andkoi in northern Afghanistan), Turkmen and Hazaras weave Aryana rugs in Islamabad Pakistan, and finish them in Lahore. These people, along with roughly one million Afghans, fled to Pakistan in 1982 to escape Afghanistan's endless civil war, and are not entirely welcome there. Pakistani police have shaken down members of Habibullah's family for money and have arbitrarily confiscated their passports. When Chris Walter met him in the 1980s, Habibullah was one of eight people living in a single room. Just 22 years old then, Habibullah was a hardworking force who pulled everyone else along. Both Habibullah and Chris Walter are thoughtful and quietly charismatic men. They are problem solvers who work very, very hard.

Turkmen weavers, whose tradition goes back hundreds of years, are among the most respected of tribal weavers. In the nineteenth century, weavers were making rugs of astonishing beauty, some with more than 400 knots per square inch and a rich palette of vegetal dyes. By 1960, Turkmen production, at least that part that reached the market, was sadly degraded. Most consisted of just two colors, red and a blue so dark it looked black, and both were made from synthetic dyes. There was little or no white to relieve the monotony of color, and the design invariably was the repeated large-gul design. When I first traveled in Afghanistan in 1971, I saw thousands of these rugs in all sizes, often stacked to the ceilings in rug stores. Afghan merchants assured us that Germans would buy them all.

Against this background, it is astonishing thirty-five years later to find Turkmen weavers, now refugees in Pakistan, weaving and exporting the exciting and beautiful rugs trade-named **Aryana** in partnership with Chris Walter. Aryanas are among my favorites in the world. They are quite decently priced: around $50 a foot. Their dyes are natural, the wool pile is handspun. In construction, Aryanas are asymmetrically knotted. Body is medium to heavy. Warp and weft are of white cotton. Their warps are somewhat-to-fully depressed. Their selvages are wool, with a single wrap. The knot-count is a sturdy, if unspectacular, 64 per square inch. Designs are eclectic: in a recent shipment of Aryanas, I saw designs modeled on northern Iranian rugs, Turkish embroideries, Caucasian rugs, the 2500-year-old Pazyric rug, a Turkmen embroidery, Turkish village rugs—everything but Chinese and Turkmen rugs. In fact, there are over 200 Aryana designs, an astonishing number when you consider that each design has to be recorded, knot for knot, and every color chosen carefully, then sampled in actual rugs, and most likely experimented with a number of times before the final version is accepted.

As guests of Habibullah and his family in Lahore, I observed firsthand how meticulously the Turkmen finish their rugs, carefully clipping and washing them, blocking them until they lie flat and straight, and reweaving any irregularities. Aryanas are consistently good. They have good quality control, good color, good finish, good designs: these are really pretty rugs. More than anything,

A prayer rug from the Ersari Turkmen Cultural Project. This small piece, about 3' by 4', is loaded with vitality and interest. It was made with natural dyes and handspun wool, and is signed and dated (top center) by the weaver. (David Holbrook Young.)

Ersari from the Ersari Turkmen Cultural Project. It is signed and dated, as are many of the rugs made by the Ersari Project. (David Holbrook Young.)

Habibullah, second from right, and the author, second from the left. Habibullah and the other Turkmen in the photograph produce Aryana rugs and carpets. Lahore, 1998.

perhaps, their artistic success is due to Mr. Walter's taste in antiques. He has chosen the best examples from the history of tribal and village weaving to model his own rugs after. Add to that a kind of controlled irregularity—and, of course, natural dyes and handspun wool—and you have rugs that are full of character. They receive a moderate finish to soften them slightly. It should be clear that I like Aryanas and recommend them enthusiastically.

A second Yayla production, called **Antique Aryanas**, have been finished to look like old rugs. If anything, they are even more attractive than regular Aryanas. But there is a trade-off. Their pile is clipped short, and the rugs are distressed to soften their colors. Foundation material is sometimes exposed on their surface. I have spoken elsewhere in this book about my uneasiness with distressing new rugs so heavily that they show wear. As a dealer, I have decided to stock no carpet so heavily antiqued that the foundation shows through. Recently Yayla has arrived at a happy compromise. Most antique Aryanas

are now clipped short enough to impart a nice old look, yet are clipped thick enough to give decades of honest service—and it is these pieces I recommend. They cost a bit more than regular Aryanas. Yayla produces two or three other lines beside Aryanas and Antique Aryanas, but they comprise a small percentage of their output. One line looks like Aryanas but is on wool foundations (white warps, brown wefts) and has double figure-of-eight selvages. Another, made by Hazaras and called (appropriately) **Hazara**, is on a wool foundation and is more finely knotted: between 100 and 120 Turkish knots per inch. I like them all.

Many rugs and carpets coming out of the camps are called **Kampbaff**, a generic name that simply means 'camp production'. We began seeing them around 1994. They have enjoyed good success in the West, and are plentiful. The first Kampbaffs were exclusively in Turkmen designs, especially the designs known as Beshir. They were dyed with attractive synthetics, often with brownish-red fields.

An Aryana prayer rug. It is quite small: about 2' by 3', a mere mat. But I think it has that x-factor that makes some rugs special. Evidently it is based on an old Turkish prayer rug, possibly a Konia. Aryana mats are my favorites; my wife and I collect them. (David Holbrook Young.)

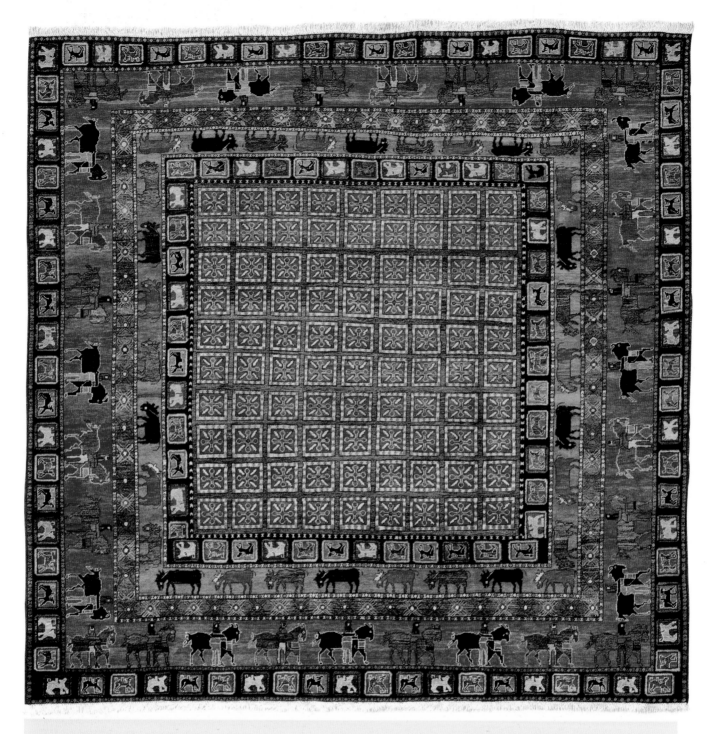

An Aryana version of the oldest known complete carpet: the Pazyric, which has been carbon dated to 500 BC. Woven by Turkmen weavers in Pakistan, Aryanas are eclectic in design. This carpet is about 10' by 11'. From the collection of Jim and Becky Eisen, Berkeley. (Don Tuttle.)

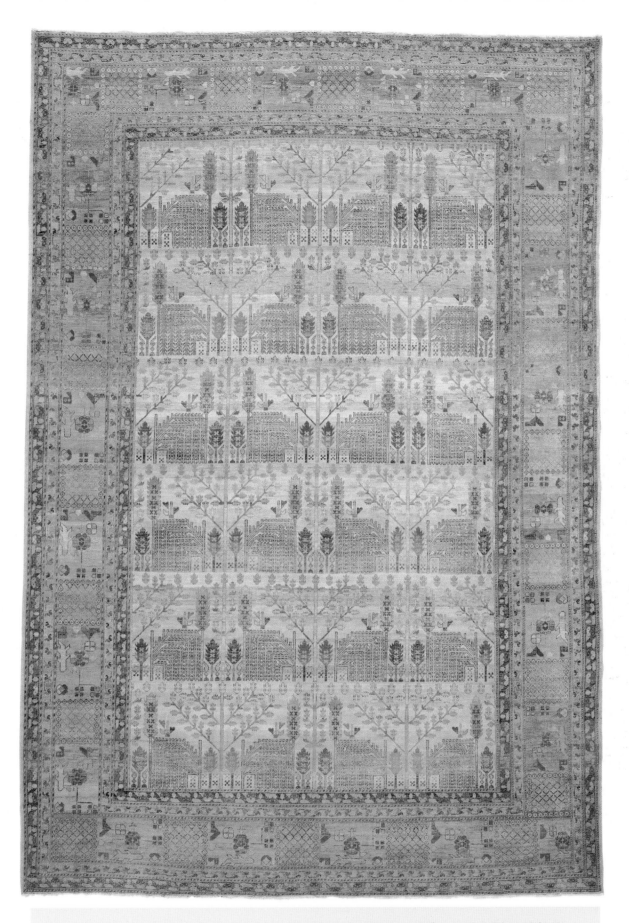

Some Aryana rugs are finished to look old, and these are called Antique Aryanas. This magnificent example, about 12' by 18', fooled Don Tuttle, the photographer who took its picture. Mr. Tuttle, who has photographed many hundreds of antique Oriental rugs, worked closely with the carpet for over an hour and assumed all the while that it was an antique. The carpet's design is one of my favorites: cypress and weeping willow trees.

A rug woven by Afghan Hazara refugees in the Pakistani camps. Only lately have rugs by Hazara weavers been distinguished from similar rugs. Its signature technical feature is a Turkish knot. This piece, fashioned from a Caucasian model, has handspun wool pile, natural dyes, and a wool foundation. (David Holbrook Young.)

Most have distinctive end finishes: two or three inches of ornamented kilims at either end. At first the Kampbaffs were heavy-bodied, but gradually the production began to be copied widely in the camps and quality suffered. Soon the weave was flabbier, and I believe the quality of wool was compromised as well. I quit buying all but the very heaviest when one I sold was returned in trade a mere three years later showing wear—a lot of wear. At the very end of the 1990s, manufacturers now produce Kampbaff rugs mostly in Caucasian designs. The best are quite good, woven now with natural dyes, handspun wool, and having excellent body. Others, though attractive, are clipped very thin and will not wear well. In any case, their prices are low—often no more than $25 per square foot.

One of the most interesting of all rugmakers is **Mason Purcell**, of **Purcell Oriental Rug Company, Ltd.** Mason Purcell is a whirlwind of energy and ideas; she speaks and thinks faster than I can hear. One of my great challenges in researching this book was gearing myself up to something approaching her pace in order to converse with her. She is an adventurer. I asked how she found the nerve to travel in Afghanistan, starting in 1975. Kipling, she said: she began reading him at age ten, and always knew she would spend part of her life in the 'Northwest Frontier'. Hers was a family of explorers. She didn't let them down. After taking a degree in textile design and dye chemistry in Virginia in 1973, she opened her own retail business in Charlottesville. In 1975 she began traveling in Afghanistan. Mason Purcell and I did not meet in Afghanistan during those years, but we easily could have. Both of us were frequent guests at the convivial table of Abdul Wassi Noorsher. Noorsher, now a busy refugee in India and else-where, was in those days a rug store owner who always seemed at the center of everything. Many young American and European rug dealers broke bread at his table. I nearly died after eating a delicious-looking tomato at Noorsher's, through no fault of his. Ms. Purcell at first combed Afghanistan for good old rugs, traveling not the 'hippie route', as she called it, but the 'rug route'. The war in Afghanistan restricted where she could travel and cut off access to rugs. Eventually she made Peshawar in Pakistan her staging base for forays into Afghanistan. Peshawar had become a center for the vast camps of Afghan refugees. With the idea of helping the refugees,

and to compensate for the diminished access to old Afghan rugs, she conceived the idea of commissioning rugs to be made in the camps in antique Turkmen designs and natural dyes. 'My initial foray can be summarized by a favorite Afghan statement, which, to this day, still sets me to screaming: "We don't do it that way." The obvious response, "Then why did you take a contract to do so?", would draw a blank look, or a vague comment like, "This is better." The financial and emotional cost of developing the production to the point I wanted was hideous.'

Ms. Purcell's first production ground rule: No person under 15 could work at her looms. Unlike men, who are not allowed around women weavers, Ms. Purcell can inspect not only the weaving but also the weavers themselves. Any girl looking too young gets sacked.

Now, after years of improving her production (she lives in Peshawar five months of the year), Mason Purcell is happy with what she produces. She has 3000 looms under contract. The whole production is in natural dyes: real indigo, madder, isparuk, walnut, pomegranate, and other traditional vegetal dyes in use in Afghanistan. The wool is a mixture drawn from Merino sheep and Karakul sheep from Afghanistan. She produces two basic lines. **Gandahara** (the ancient name for Peshawar) rugs are authentic reproductions of eighteenth- and nineteenth-century Afghan designs. She says she is the first person to program archaic Turkmen designs in American sizes—a feat more difficult than you may think. Weavers are used to working in meter sizes for the European market, and resist adapting to foot sizes. Gandahara rugs are heavy-bodied, finely knotted, lively-colored and nice-feeling rugs. Her second line is called **Vintage**. Vintage rugs are modeled after old Persian pieces: Kurdish, Bijar, Hamadan, Sarab, Sultanabad, Oushak, and others. Like the Gandahara rugs, they are made with natural dyes.

One of my favorite productions from the camps is called **Halmahmadi**. (I spell this phonetically, the best I can. I have bought many of these rugs and others from Afghan friends without ever having seen the name written.) That is, they are called Halmahmadi now, but two or three years ago when I first saw them, they were called Khan Mohammadi. I cannot tell you who Khan Mohammadi is or was, or why the sudden evolution in his name took place (except that Halmahmadi is easier to say). I am

Mason Purcell among Afghan refugee friends in Pakistan.

equally puzzled about where their designs spring from. They are recognizably Turkmen in character, but unlike any Turkmen designs I have seen. These rugs are characterized by their usually coppery-colored fields, by their highly lustrous finish, their usually clean, neat, and tidy appearance, and by the decorative, flat-woven finish on both ends. Typically, they are heavier-bodied and finer-knotted than Kampbaff rugs. They are, to me, a welcome departure from the typical red, large-gul Afghan rugs that for decades were almost the only Turkmen rugs available. Like so many of the rugs in the market now that I admire, just four or five years ago they weren't made. Most sizes are available, though it is very hard to find a true 8 by 10 or 9 by 12. They retail for roughly $30 per square foot—a bargain, I think. Some Halmahmadis do have one problem, however. Those finished (chemically) in Pakistan often have wool fringe that is brittle and which breaks easily.

This results in premature wear of the fringe, which will be annoying to many owners, though not fatal to the rugs. Others have been finished in Germany with better results. Their fringes are strong. You can test the fringes yourself simply by stressing them.

There are now several relatively small manufacturers of natural-dyed rugs in Pakistan who show signs of becoming major players. **Art Resources** is one of my favorites. Art Resources is a Los Angeles business run by Iranian-born **Jack Simantob**. Equipped with an MBA from an American college and a good background in antique rugs, Mr. Simantob first imported rugs from Pakistan and then began to make them. His vision was different from other rugmakers in one important respect. He wanted to create great, old-looking rugs, but he wanted to do it without distressing them with chemicals or other methods which

Previous Pages:

A detail from a Gandahara by Mason Purcell. This piece is woven with natural dyes and handspun wool by Afghan refugees in Pakistan.

A Vintage rug by Mason Purcell. Rugs in this line are fashioned after old Persian pieces. This carpet most likely was based on an old Persian Bijar.

Halmahmadi (or Khan Mohammadi) rug from the Pakistani refugee camps, made by Turkmen weavers. These rugs seem to constitute a new genre. Their designs look Turkmen, but I had not seen them before about 1994. They have chrome dyes, silky, machine-spun wool pile, and a nice appearance. Occasionally their wool fringe breaks down, apparently the result of bleaching in the finishing process. You can test the fringe by pulling on it. This rug is about 3' by 5', but Halmahmadis are available up to 10' by 14' in a number of designs. (David Holbrook Young.)

A new rug from Art Resources, based on an old Turkish Ushak. It perfectly epitomizes what is meant by 'decorative carpet'. Natural dyes, handspun wool.

A rug based on an old Heriz, from Art Resources. It is new, but its appearance would lead most to assume it is old. It is just as attractive as if it were. It is about 4½′ by 5½′, naturally dyed and with handspun wool pile.

compromise the quality of the wool. He ages his rugs 'naturally', as he says, and over a period of months. That approach is well-nigh heroic when you consider how expensive it must be to tie up scores of large rugs for months while they age. Still, the price to the end user is a bit less than most other 'antiqued' rugs—about $55 per square foot—and I have to say that the wool pile in the Art Resources rugs feels much better than wool in rugs that have been aged overnight. I did not at first ask Mr. Simantob what his 'natural aging' consists of, assuming the answer is a professional secret, but at the risk of being rude, eventually I did inquire. I was right the first time: professional secret. But we did discuss the aging process commonly used in Pakistan. By his account, the most frequent formulation is called Kachipaki, a mixture of half chemicals and half soap. The chemicals include a disinfectant that apparently has a distressing effect on wool (desirable if it is your intent to distress wool), plus a fabric softener that serves to open pores of the wool fibers, making them more receptive to other chemicals. Jack Simantob flatly refuses to use these or any other chemicals; he strongly believes that nearly all hurt wool. His end product is a new rug with short pile and an old look, which yet has healthy wool. With about 230 looms at his command, he cannot meet the present demand for his rugs; they are all spoken for long before they come off the loom. But look for Art Resources to become one of the major manufacturers of our era.

As we have seen, one facet of the rug renaissance is the huge variety of rugs in the market. In part this is accounted for by the ease with which would-be manufacturers can attain their wish. The refugee camps in Pakistan are especially accessible to them. A gentleman named **Homayoon Mosenpour** is a good example of someone who started small and is in the process of growing. In 1987 he came to the U.S. as a refugee from Afghanistan, where he had been a weaver and repairer of rugs. He settled in Monterey, California where he became involved with antique rugs. In 1994, he traveled to Pakistan to visit fellow immigrants in the camps, and wound up spending the only money he had ($3000) to have rugs made there. He was proud to call his new business **Hazara Looms**—proud because he is a member of one of Afghanistan's ethnic minorities called the Hazara. When he decided to produce rugs with natural dyes, he was able to draw upon information and materials gathered in Kabul, Afghanistan in about 1985 by the United Nations in a program designed to revive their use among Afghan weavers. Today, Hazara Looms controls about 180 looms. Homayoon Mosenpour is involved in every step of the rugmaking process. His carpets are among my favorites. They have the soft look of old rugs, and the softness has been achieved without any harm to the rugs themselves. I believe Hazara Looms will become a major force in the natural dye carpet industry. If it does, says Homayoon Mosenpour, it will not be for the sake of making money, but to promote the cause of his fellow Hazara refugees.

Just now as I am writing, a production is emerging that is startlingly good. Frustrated by the willfulness of many Turkish weavers, Turkish-born and educated **Izi Mizrahi** of **I. M. International**, who has produced rugs in Turkey for fifteen years, is shifting much of his production to the refugee camps of Pakistan. Speaking Turkish, he has been able to communicate with Turkmen weavers, whom he has selected to work on his 600 looms in Pakistan. Drawing upon the wisdom of his fifteen years in Turkey, Mr. Mizrahi in a mere two years has begun turning out magnificent carpets in old Persian and Caucasian designs and in natural dyes and handspun wool. They have an old look, accomplished without distressing or compromising their wool, or over-softening their dyes in the finishing process. Still, I will not be fully satisfied until I see at least one of these pieces finished with absolutely no wash. I suspect that they are so good that they will stand on their own with no 'help' at all. Though production is still small, it is possible that Izi Yumurtaci's Persian-designed carpets from Pakistan are the best in the world. They sell for about $75 per square foot.

A rug from Hazara Looms. It was made by Hazara weavers with natural dyes and handspun wool in Pakistan. About 5' by 7'.

Pakistani Sultanabad by I. M. International. This production came on the market shortly before the book went to press. At this moment, at least, these carpets are arguably the best in the world. I am not exaggerating when I say that we witness improvements in the rugs of this era every day. About 8' 7" by 11' 8". (Don Tuttle.)

Chapter 7

The Rugs and Carpets of India

In 1993, India exported $170 million worth of carpets to the United States. Yet rug collectors and even many rug dealers know almost nothing about the rug industry in India. My early education in Oriental rugs came at a time when Indian rugs were considered not quite real, and rug books barely gave them a mention. Like many other old-school rug collectors, I can draw a map of Iran (whose rugs have not crossed American borders in appreciable quantities for nearly twenty years), argue price in Farsi, and discuss obscure Persian villages. But I was appallingly uninformed about Indian rug production.

Like Pakistan, India is not generally supposed to have a rugmaking tradition. No such misunderstanding should survive the superb exhibition of Mughal carpets of the late sixteenth through the eighteenth centuries mounted in 1998 at the Metropolitan Museum of Art in New York. Though Mughal rug designers were certainly influenced by Persian court rugs, they also appear to have emulated the designs of rugs indigenous to northwest India. Mughal carpets are not merely Persian rugs woven in India; they have their own discernibly Indian look. Even after the Mughal Empire crumbled, weaving continued in India. The late nineteenth and early twentieth centuries saw a large production of Indian rugs and carpets in Agra, Amritsar, and elsewhere. But most contemporary rug connoisseurs deemed them corrupted by Persian influence and by Western demand and unworthy of study, so that these carpets were passed over in books. Like earlier Mughal rugs, they were clearly influenced by the rugs of Iran, but, again, they have their own look, in part due to an unusual color palette and not-quite-Persian designs. Because almost nothing was written about them, it is now nearly impossible to determine exactly where Indian carpets from the turn of the century were woven. As it happens, they are among the most desirable and expensive rugs in the decorative rug market today, but scholars, dealers, and owners have little hard information about them.

In the past, Indian rugs did not enjoy a good reputation in America. As long as Iran was the most important supplier to the U.S., India competed by manufacturing low-end rugs almost exclusively. Most such rugs made their way to department stores where they sold very inexpensively. Certain grades of Indian wool were decidedly inferior, but the Indian government, to support the Indian wool industry, insisted that native wool be used in Indian rugs. Worse still, other fibers, such as hemp, made their way into the cheapest Indian rugs. The worst examples from that period have the texture of rope. By about 1980, the government dropped the laws requiring the use of native wool in rug manufacturing, and rugmakers began to import lustrous, long-stapled wool from Australia and New Zealand. Often it is mixed with Indian wool, but sometimes it is used alone. I date this change as the beginning of India's recovery from its bad reputation.

After Persian rugs became unavailable to Americans, India responded by producing increasingly better rugs. In 1980, the finest quality rugs produced in India were woven with 90 knots per square inch. Today Indian weavers make rugs with 240 knots per square inch and more.

> In India, quality sometimes is measured in terms of knots per square inch. A 9/9 Jaipur, for instance, has 81 knots per square inch, but more often it is quantified in a different system. One typical knot-count of the second type, for instance, is 7/52. To convert this to knots per square inch, multiply 7 by 52 and divide by 4. The result is 90 knots per square inch.

During the '80s and '90s, India established its capacity to make first-rate rugs with excellent materials. Most are in Persian designs, with good synthetic dyes and machine-spun wool. They are so successful and in many cases such bargains that they have become the staple fare of rug stores and department stores throughout America. At one time, there were only a handful of designs in which Indian carpets were woven, but today there are hundreds—so many, in fact, that I can only survey a fraction of them. Because so many businesses import mainstream Indian rugs, retailers rarely mention their names to customers. These importers are essentially anonymous except within inch are so consistently good that, for the consumer, choosing from among them will come down to a matter of common sense and personal taste. A good rug should lie flat and straight. Its wool should be lively and never noticeably dry. There should be no hint of bleeding or fading in its colors, and it should have good body. Beyond that, your choice will be a matter of taste and how much you want to spend.

The **Henry Gertmenian Company** of San Francisco is one my favorite importers of mainstream Indian rugs (along with much else. The company is discussed further in Chapter Ten on Chinese rugs). **Al Gertmenian**, who gave up a law practice to join the family carpet business in 1980, is one of those rare souls who radiate honesty. In the company, he is in charge of importing rugs from India. During the early '80s he would examine dozens of lines, and be happy to find one he liked well enough to buy. At the hotel that night he would wonder who in the world bought the other ones—the rugs he passed over. Today, of fifteen lines of rugs he examines, he may like twelve. He agrees that we are enjoying a golden age of Oriental rugs, and one of its features, he says, is the sheer number and diversity of good products available. In part, he attributes the healthy diversity of rugs in India to the fact that for the past four or five years German demand has been soft, stimulating India to cater to the more demanding American market. But Al Gertmenian predicts that, when German demand reasserts itself, India's willingness to experiment and try new ideas will yield to more mainstream production. Like many importers, he is wary of the present market's fickleness. At one time he believed that his business would do well if he had ten good lines of Indian rugs available in a number of color combinations and in all sizes. Today, he realizes, demand changes so fast that the 'ten good lines' approach can never work. The trick now is to stay on top of changing fashions. The Henry Gertmenian Company currently offers the very decorative carpets called **9/9 Jaipur** and other natural-dyed rugs. (He is skeptical, by the way, that 9/9 Jaipurs are in fact vegetal-dyed. He absolutely could not pin down his producers on the subject.) But I find Mr. Gertmenian's more standard imports to be most characteristic of the Gertmenian approach. The rugs I am speaking of have withstood the test of time. They have universal appeal, will not soon grow unfashionable, and are durable, honest rugs offered at fair prices. Among my favorites is his **Indo-Kashan Vase Rug** in an all-over design inspired by sixteenth-century Persian prototypes.

9/9 Jaipurs were introduced to retailers just several years ago, yet in a short time they have become immensely popular. '9/9 Jaipur', by which they are known in the trade, refers to the knot count (81 per square inch) and the Indian city in which they are manufactured. Canny marketers—or perhaps hundreds of retailers on their own initiative—have succeeded in making them known to the public as **tea-dyed** or **tea-washed rugs**. Fair enough. Though not actually dyed with tea, they are washed in tea and henna in the finish. At first, retailers were told by manufacturers that 'tea-washed' carpets were made with natural dyes, and that is the impression these carpets make. But many of us became skeptical, and now it is apparent that all but a very few 9/9 Jaipurs are made with synthetic dyes. These synthetically dyed rugs, however, are washed with natural dyes (including tea) in the finishing process. Typically, tea-washed rugs are clipped quite thick and have huge body. They are woven with low-contrast, soft colors in designs that are more European than Asian. Most are made with some percentage of New Zealand mixed with Indian wool. Their general impression is Victorian: formal, shadowy, European, sophisticated. Are they good rugs? I think so. They certainly have plenty of heft and wool good enough to see them through decades of use on the floor. And they have an important place in the decorative rug market, which likes soft colors and low contrast. I value those which are not too murky, not too clouded by tea, henna, and whatnot. Rugs should glow a little, so the more New Zealand wool and the less dulling of the colors with tea, the better. Though perhaps subject to criticism for not being very traditional in design, tea-dyed Jaipurs are different, interesting, and fun. They are also fairly pricey: usually about $60, but ranging from $45 to nearly $100 a foot. An example is illustrated on page 142.

Indo-Kashan. Indian rugs with chrome dyes and machine-spun wool pile are perhaps the most widely imported Oriental rugs in America. Most collectors of old rugs sneer at them. But the best of them, of which this 12 by 18-foot carpet is a perfect example, are excellent and beautiful rugs that, in my opinion, are destined to become valuable antiques. This carpet was based on a Persian Kashan that, in turn was based on sixteenth-century Persian vase carpets. Imported by the Henry Gertmenian Company of San Francisco. (Don Tuttle.)

Teddy Sumner and **George Jevremovic** were the first people to make rugs on a commercial scale in modern India with natural dyes and handspun wool. Mr. Sumner studied painting as a fine arts major in Seattle (when pressed he admits to being 'a painter with a small "p"') then joined his family's carpet business, Michaelian and Kohlberg, in New York. His grandfather, Frank Michaelian, was active in the business in the '20s and '30s, when travel to and from the source of rugs was by steamship, and travel in the East itself was often by camel. By his own admission, when Teddy Sumner joined the business in 1982 he was too uninformed about rugs to be intimidated by the prospect of making them. Within a short time he began producing Aubusson-inspired needlepoint rugs in China (discussed in Chapter Nine). By 1985, he was importing carpets from Nepal. At some point he had become aware of the Azeri rugs George Jevremovic was making in Turkey with natural dyes, and, inspired by them, he began to experiment with natural dyes in India. Quite likely he was the first American to do so, and at a time when probably no Indians were using natural dyes except, perhaps, as hobbyists. At this point, in 1990, he and George Jevremovic (who is discussed in detail in Chapter Five) became partners in a business called **Black Mountain Looms**, which ultimately became the first full, natural-dye production in India. Rather than take credit for being a pioneer of natural dyeing, Teddy Sumner treats his accomplishments rather lightly. 'It was not that complicated. We found a good book on indigenous natural dyes and plenty of reference material. Working with natural dyes, after all, is not rocket science.' On the other hand, organizing Indians to spin wool by hand was a challenge. The difficulty the partners encountered was ironic in view of Mahatma Gandhi's famous promotion of hand spinning, which he recommended to his countrymen as a path to self-reliance. No one in India seemed to have retained the skill. Finally, Messieurs Sumner and Jevremovic applied for help to an organization devoted to keeping Gandhi's ideas alive, and they found several older women who could still spin. Black Mountain Looms asked them to train thousands of other Indians in the art, and Teddy Sumner and George Jevremovic were then ready to start production. The partners had interests in common, but they especially looked forward to benefiting from their different backgrounds in the business. Eventually they collaborated in productions in India, Turkey, Eastern Europe, and China, and their rugs are among the best each of these countries produces.

Teddy Sumner of Michaelian & Kohlberg (on right) and George Jevremovic of Woven Legends are the partners behind Black Mountain Looms.

Mahindra, made by Black Mountain Looms. There are so many great Mahindras that I agonized over which to illustrate. This Mahindra is based on a Persian Vase Carpet, just as are the Henry Gertmenian carpet, the Old World Classics carpet, and the Noble House carpet by Samad Brothers—all of which you will find pictured in this chapter. It is interesting to compare them and to note the fluidity and spaciousness of this Mahindra. Its designers have made excellent color choices.

This Mahindra looks like it might be a detail from an old pictorial Mughal carpet. Whether or not I am correct, it is true that today's rug designers often create their rugs from enlarged details of old rugs, thereby producing carpets with large, dramatic designs. This rug has a wonderful feeling of playfulness and naivete.

A Mahindra from Black Mountain Looms, made in India. This carpet, based on an old Bijar design from Iran, is crooked. Whether that is a fatal flaw, a pleasant irregularity, or a matter of little importance is a matter for each to decide. Notice the unusual green border.

(As a result of his association with George Jevremovic, Teddy Sumner says, he has come to see carpets differently—with the focus less on design than on the materials as ends in themselves. Details of the border, for instance, may shrink in importance compared to a carpet's luscious wool, or gorgeous natural dyes. It is interesting to me that people looking at the same rug can see it quite differently. Haynes Robinson, an importer discussed below, sees things differently still. He pictures a rug in a room, in reference to its setting. *Seeing* rugs differently, do Teddy Sumner and Haynes Robinson make rugs that *look* different? Compare their rugs for yourself as they are represented by the plates in this chapter.)

Black Mountain Looms' production in India is called **Mahindra**, and it has been powerfully influential in the industry. It appeared at a time when Indian rugs were faulted for their lack of character—for being too regular, too stiff. Mahindras were truly revolutionary. Often in designs found in no other carpets during the past sixty years, they are woven with natural dyes and handspun wool on cotton foundations. Warps are completely depressed. There are about 130 Persian knots per square inch. Most of their designs are based on unusual Persian city rugs, though a few seem to be based on old Indian rugs such as Agras. Today a few other manufacturers have captured the look of Mahindras, and others have knocked off their designs knot for knot. But Mahindras still are the leaders in a field created by Black Mountain Looms.

A familiar name resurfaces in India at this point in our story, **Chris Walter**. We have seen that Mr. Walter was the pioneer of natural dyeing in Pakistan and that, besides producing rugs in Pakistan, he created a natural dye production in Nepal—perhaps the only production there exclusively of natural-dyed rugs. I only recently became aware that Chris Walter also brought to life natural-dyed rugs in India, beginning in 1992, just a year or two after Black Mountain Looms founded the first natural dye workshop there. He allied himself with three Indian brothers who had not before made knotted carpets: Nabullah, Habibullah, and Ansari Aswam from Badhooi. Chris Walter taught them methods of rugmaking and dyeing that he had learned in his other projects. Together they began weaving rugs that Mr. Walter calls **Zamin** (with

the accent on the second syllable.) Brother Nabullah was electrocuted in a tragic accident, and his death added to the difficulties in perfecting the new production. But by 1998 the rugs had matured, and today they are a wonderful addition to the renaissance in Oriental rugs. There are two grades of Zamins: one has about 65 knots per square inch, the other about 100 (I have counted an actual 130 in one piece). Both are unquestioned bargains—likely the best buys in the world for natural-dyed, handspun-wool rugs and carpets, at between $25 (!) and $38 a square foot. Theirs is 100% New Zealand wool—but with an important distinction. In the production of Zamins, New Zealand wool is received 'raw', then *hand-carded* and spun by hand. No one recognizes these rugs as Indian; they look and feel completely different. Most Indian carpets are woven with very thick wefts, and thus have a stiff and heavy 'handle'. Zamins also have huge body, but it is achieved by packing wool pile densely into the rug. Zamins are eclectic in design, drawing for inspiration from Iran, Turkey, and elsewhere. They are colorful, 'villagey' in character, studies in natural dye, and—don't forget—only about $2000 to $3000 for an 8 by 10-foot carpet. I could not recommend them more highly. The catch? There aren't many of them.

Rugs by Robinson was founded by a young man from Atlanta named Haynes Robinson. His mother was an interior designer, and Mr. Robinson began work in partnership with her, importing Portuguese needlepoint rugs and selling them to the designer trade. They started business with eight pieces. By 1990 they felt that Portuguese needlepoint rugs had become too expensive, and the business began to import needlepoint rugs from China instead. By the next year they were operating as wholesalers. At the same time, the Robinsons had added antique rugs and carpets to their inventory, becoming known for their collection of Ushaks. Haynes Robinson had become familiar with Mahindra rugs from India, produced by George Jevremovic and Teddy Sumner in natural dyes after Persian designs, and he began to look for a producer in India who could help him with something similar. By 1993, he found one who was already weaving with natural dyes and who had developed a good wash. He asked that the wash be cut in half, and submitted drawings of classic

This wonderful carpet from Rugs by Robinson of Atlanta, Georgia, in many ways represents the state of the art of decorative carpets in our rug renaissance. Color choices are excellent (they are made from natural dyes), the drawing is excellent, the finish of the rug (the way its surface looks) is unsurpassed, and it has huge body. The design is pleasantly irregular. It is about 10' by 12' and part of the Robinson Revival series. (Don Tuttle.)

Another blockbuster carpet from Rugs by Robinson. I am not certain on what old rug it was based—most likely an old Agra from India—but, in a way, it is not important. Robinson designers change designs and colors to suit their taste. This carpet is from Robinson's Revival collection.

'Dream Collection' carpet from Samad Brothers of Secaucus, New Jersey. Dream collection rugs, though there are many different designs in the series, have a recognizable character, associated more with European than Middle Eastern or Asian design. They are available in most sizes. Chrome dyes, mill-spun wool, very heavy body.

A 'Noble House' carpet from Samad Brothers. This and other Noble House rugs are among the very best in the market. It is heavy and sturdy and should last for three quarters of a century. Its materials are first rate: natural dyes, good wool pile. But, above all, it is gorgeous: full of interest and character. Though its abrash (horizontal bands of differing color) is strong—maybe even radical—it works, making us feel like we won't again see a carpet quite like this one—which we won't. Its prototype is an antique Vase Carpet.

Indian rugs such as Agras. A short while later he was able to introduce his famed **Revival** line of rugs, showing them in Atlanta in 1994.

It is interesting to me that Haynes Robinson entered the business with a designer's perspective. He told me that when he looks at a rug, he judges it by the way it will look in a room. (I have become aware that my wife and I see quite different things when we look at Oriental rugs together. She sees rugs just as Mr. Robinson described: in terms of their effect, i.e. according to how they will look in a room. I believe that, because of my old-rug background, I see them first in relation to their prototype, and then simply in their own terms rather than in a context.) Haynes Robinson's carpets reflect his designer's eye. If there is such a thing as designer colors, his rugs have them. But it is the beauty of his Revival rugs' surfaces that is extraordinary. The wool glows and feels wonderful to the touch; the surfaces have a feeling of depth. Surprisingly, most Revivals are woven with machine-spun wool, which promotes a formal look. But that is balanced by intelligent use of abrash and asymmetry. Revival carpets look old, yet they are in full pile, not distressed. Few have been able to match the finish his producer has achieved, and no one has bettered it. Revival rugs are one-of-a-kind, or nearly so. The same design is produced more than once, but colors vary so greatly from one rug to another that they are not really alike. New rugs as individualistic as his Revival rugs must be bought and sold like antiques. Unfortunately, they are nearly as expensive as antiques: Revival pieces sell for about $95 per square foot. Rugs by Robinson is constantly producing new lines of carpets—all of them are worthy.

Three of the most eloquent gentlemen in the Oriental rug business are **David Samad**, **Malcolm Samad**, and **Thomas Franklin**, their national sales manager. David and Malcolm Samad established **Samad Brothers Oriental Rugs** in New York in 1985—an auspicious date, I believe, with which I associate the beginning of the renaissance of Oriental rugs, or when it began to show up in America, anyway. Their first shop was established in only 400 square feet. During the earliest days of the business, an Indian supplier held back half of a shipment, afraid to trust the brothers who were not well known. Two years later they moved to Secaucus, New Jersey and occupied a 3000-square-foot space. For the first ten years or so the brothers dealt in a variety of Chinese and Indian rugs. They were drawn to Jaipur in India largely because most other importers were not, and there, in the mid-1990s, they were introduced to what may be the only Indian family producing carpets on their own initiative with natural dyes. The introduction resulted in a relationship that made Oriental rug history. From it were born the famous Dream Collection and Noble House carpets that rival any made in the past eighty years. Malcolm and David Samad are not interested in literally reproducing antique rugs. Instead, they give their Indian producers designs of antique rugs as starting points from which weavers can improvise, and give them specific colors with which to work. The resulting carpets are unlike any made before. In terms the Samad brothers use, their carpets are 'recreations—not reproductions'. They re-create old carpets (a process that involves creativity) rather than merely copy them.

The **Dream Collection** rugs were unveiled in 1996 in eight patterns. Today there are thirty-nine copyrighted patterns from classical or original designs. They are made to be reproducible, but steps are taken to give each carpet an individual character. Though synthesized Swiss dyes are used, they are dyed in small batches to prevent too great a uniformity of colors. A blend of wools is spun together by hand, giving the surface of each carpet a slight nubby quality and a lot of character. They sell for roughly $80 per square foot.

The **Noble House** carpets are made two-on-a-loom, never again to be produced exactly the same. Small batches of natural dyes are used in these carpets on mill-spun New Zealand Wool. Like some other carpets made in Jaipur, both Noble House and Dream Collection rugs are made with brown, wool wefts. All other Indian rugs I can think of are made with cotton wefts. Noble House carpets sell for about $95 per square foot. Their finish sets standards for the industry, so I asked how it was achieved. Malcolm and David Samad cheerfully pleaded ignorance. 'It's better that I don't know,' said David Samad, perhaps secure in the assurance that, even if brutally tortured, he could be trusted never to surrender the secret formula.

This carpet was made by a relatively small and new company called Old World Classics, from natural dyes and handspun wool. I feel the world is fortunate that rugs this good did not die out seventy years ago. There is a problem though: Old World Classics is able to produce only a handful of carpets like this each year. A shortage of the best carpets is one of the persistent problems of our era. This rug was based on Safavid period vase carpets and is about 9' by 12'.

A blue-field Indian Sarouk imported by Haroonian International. Haroonian calls rugs in this line 'Claridge'. These are the first really Sarouk-like new carpets that I have seen woven in India or anywhere else. In particular, they are like Persian Sarouks of the '20s and '30s.

As we have seen elsewhere, George Jevremovic of Woven Legends was influenced by Harald Böhmer of the DOBAG project. Teddy Sumner of Michaelian and Kohlberg was influenced by George Jevremovic. Hanes Robinson of Rugs by Robinson was influenced by both Teddy Sumner and George Jevremovic. So were many others, including a young man named Berislav Kuntic. Mr. Kuntic began his career in rugs in 1987 as a stock clerk in George Jevremovic's business Woven Legends, surrounded by a stimulating mixture of antique rugs, the first Azeri productions, and a lot of exciting conversation about Oriental rugs. Soon the Croatian-born Mr. Kuntic managed Woven Legend's New York office. After five years with Woven Legends, Berislav Kuntic moved on to ABC, the country's largest retailer of Oriental rugs, where he worked in sales. In his four and a half years at ABC, he became more and more interested in producing rugs, and eventually left to establish **Old World Classics**. Convinced that demand was increasing for finer-knotted rugs and more refined-looking rugs than those produced in Turkey (where Azeris are made), he began production in India in about 1995. Today, along with an Indian partner, he controls about 120 looms. I count him among the new breed of manufacturers who are true rugmakers, involved in every step of the process. But heroes are made, not born, and he is having to work out the significant problems inherent in making rugs with natural dyes. To their horror, one experiment that he and his partner tried with dyes turned twenty finished carpets purple. But each time I see rugs from Old World Classics they are better than before. They are Mahindra-like rugs and carpets in about forty designs, made with handspun wool and natural dyes, and washed and finished entirely without chemicals.

For decades, Americans have imported Indian rugs called **Sarouks** or **Indo-Sarouks**, though they have borne little resemblance to the Persian rugs after which they are named. Now we are beginning to see Indo-Sarouks worthy of the name. **Lee Haroonian** of **Haroonian Rugs International** imports a line called **Claridge** that includes really impressive examples. They illustrate how successful rugs still can be in chrome dyes and mill-spun wool.

It is appropriate to end our survey of Indian carpets by mentioning once more the mainstream rugs you will find in the market. You will see 1000 of them for every natural-dyed Indian rug. It is my feeling that even **inexpensive Indian rugs** today are far better than they were ten years ago. Almost invariably the wool on today's cheap rugs is better than yesterday's, and an effort is made now to introduce character into even quite inexpensive pieces. It is astonishing to me that the Indians can weave, let us say, an 8 by 10 foot carpet that is destined to give forty or fifty years of good, honest service underfoot, is really attractive, and can sell in America for less than $2800—without resorting to child labor.

A red-field variant of Haroonian International's Claridge Sarouk.

Chapter 8

The Rugs and Carpets of Afghanistan

At the end of the 1990s, it is very hard to sort out which 'Afghan' goods are actually made in Afghanistan, and which are made in Pakistan by Afghan refugees. At least a million Afghans, including hundreds of thousands of rug-weavers, fled Afghanistan during its war with the Soviet Union and its subsequent civil war, settling especially in Pakistan and Iran. To my knowledge, no rugs are shipped directly from Afghanistan to the United States or Europe today. Instead, they are transported to Pakistan, then shipped abroad. So both Afghan rugs made in Pakistan, and Afghan rugs made in Afghanistan, are shipped from Pakistan, making it usually impossible to sort out where a particular Afghan rug is actually woven. Perhaps it doesn't really matter. Presumably at some time many of the refugees will return to Afghanistan and resume rug-making there. For the purposes of this book, we will assume that all rugs made by Afghans not known to have been produced elsewhere were made in Afghanistan.

In relation to the West, most Afghan villages really are remote. They have been made even less accessible by incessant war. Consequently, Afghan weavers have not been subject to much pressure from Western markets to produce rugs for Western tastes. Most Afghan weavers make rugs that are about the same as those they have woven for decades. That is the good news, and the bad: good because it is, after all, pleasing that some weavers have retained ties to their own traditions, but bad because the products of the past several decades to which weavers have remained faithful are far inferior to earlier weavings. I cannot say that weavers in Afghanistan have contributed greatly to the rug renaissance, but, goodness knows, that is understandable in light of the chaotic conditions brought on by the invasion of the Soviet Union in the 1970s and Afghanistan's subsequent, interminable civil war. In any case, Afghan rugs are genuine, often charming—and always phenomenally inexpensive.

The quintessential Afghan rug of the past fifty years is a wool-on-wool product with a repeated octagonal figure (often inaccurately called elephant's foot) on a red field. In the trade it is called simply **Afghan** or **Dulatabad**. Afghans are made by Turkmen weavers in northern Afghanistan. A hundred years ago the guls (as the octagonal figures are properly called) were large—often 16 inches wide in bigger rugs. Guls have become smaller over the years until today they most often are no more than several inches across. As the guls have shrunk, so has the range of colors in the rugs. Today most Afghans contain only two colors: a rather bright red and a blue so deep that it looks black. Still, Afghans have survived because they are basically so appealing. They are still popular with Afghan people, including the many who have emigrated to the West.

One of the most exotic and distinctive of all Oriental rugs is the **Shindand** or **Adraskand** (named after neighboring villages), woven near Harat in western Afghanistan. Strangely elongated human and animal figures are their signature look.

Another staple of Afghanistan is **Baluchi rugs**, most notably **Baluchi prayer rugs**. Made by Baluchi people, especially in western Afghanistan near Herat, Baluchi prayer rugs can be muddy-looking rugs of almost no merit, or charming little tribal rugs. Virtually all are made on wool foundations with synthetic dyes, and measure about 2' 8" by 4' 7". In recent years I have had occasion to look through container loads of five or six thousand pieces to pick out my favorite two hundred. The best have lustrous wool, good body, balanced color, stable dyes, and interesting designs. At around $200 each, they seem like great bargains to me.

A new genre of rug has appeared in the past fifteen years: the **Baluchi War Rug**. These rugs, which may be nearly any dimension but are usually prayer-rug size, depict scenes from the everyday life of the Afghan people. Sadly, of late that means scenes involving fighter planes, helicopters, machine guns, troop transports, and the like. We tend to think of Oriental rug design as locked in tradition,

The classic 'Afghan' rug with large guls. This piece is a great improvement over the Afghans of the recent past. It was made by weavers of the Ersari Turkmen Cultural Survival project in natural dyes and with handspun wool. (David Holbrook Young.)

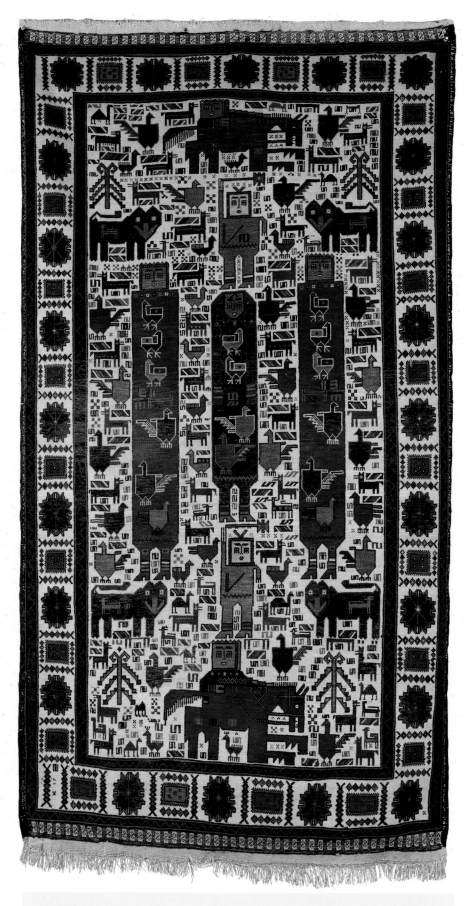

Adraskand rug from Afghanistan, about 3 by 6'. Adraskands are among the most interesting rugs produced in Afghanistan, with their peculiar, elongated human and animal figures. Often their dyes bleed when exposed to water, and many of these charming rugs have been spoiled. (David Holbrook Young.)

Belouch Prayer Rug. Columns, spires, minarets and rooftops all ascend, giving this prayer rug a strong directional orientation. Muslim worshipers point their rugs toward Mecca during prayer. Though many Belouch prayer rugs are woven for export, somehow they do not feel cranked out. There is a genuine tribal or village feeling in nearly every Afghan rug.

passed down from mother to daughter. Certainly everything about making rugs in the Middle East and Asia is conservative. Techniques and designs are slow to change, and no rugmaker is sitting beside her tent 'doing her own thing'. But rug-design is not static, cast in stone forevermore by some progenitor. Witness the war rugs. To me, the miracle of these pieces is that weavers are able to incorporate bizarre elements into them, such as machine guns, and they still manage to look like Oriental rugs! But it must be said that most, and possibly all, are made with dyes and materials of dubious quality.

Afghanistan has always produced an abundance of kilims and still does. It does seem, though, as if the diversity reaching the West is far less now than it was two decades ago. One type is produced in enormous quantity: the ubiquitous **Maimana kilim** from the north. Maimanas are sold in prodigious numbers in America, especially in Santa Fe, New Mexico, where they resonate to the South West architecture and lifestyle. Maimanas are woven in a slit-tapestry weave, a type of kilim weaving that leaves characteristic small (up to three-quarters of an inch) gaps or slits between areas where one color leaves off and another begins. Their wool is rather coarse. In nearly thirty years I have seen only one that I was certain was made from natural dyes. They come in most sizes, though true 8 by 10s and 9 by 12s are rare. Maimanas are phenomenally inexpensive-from $6 to $10 per sq. ft.-but care should be taken in choosing them. At worst, they are murky-looking things with runny dyes, scratchy, lusterless wool, a loose weave, and areas of bright, clearly synthetic dye—and at the very worst they smell alarmingly of dung—presumably due to unwise choices in the finishing process. At best, they have good body, clear, harmonious color, good wool, and a pleasant aspect.

There is a small quantity of finely knotted rugs on silk foundations in the market, some with wool pile and others with silk. These are often called **silk-warp Mauris**. I have known for years that these pieces are made in the capital city of Kabul in a workshop on Chicken Street, but only recently have I learned that they are (or at least were) made by Hazara weavers, and in particular by relatives of a gentleman well known and respected in Kabul: Haji Yusef. In 1985, the United Nations sponsored a natural dye project in Kabul and these rugs probably evolved from that project. One line of silk-warp Mauris is made in classic Turkmen Dulatabad designs with very small guls. Another line, usually with a silk pile as well as a silk foundation, is in designs that suggest the architecture of mosques. I see others whose designs are a mystery to me. They are often impressive rugs, but one must examine many of them to find one that is 100 percent pleasing.

Hundreds of Afghan immigrants (or refugees-I don't know which to call them) living in the U.S. are involved in the Oriental rug business, and many frequent the Middle East in search of merchandise. Most buy rugs from the Pakistani camps and import them into America. A few are now involved in designing rugs themselves and commissioning them to be made in Pakistan. One such

Afghan-American is **Ahmad Ahmadi** from **Ariana Rugs and Kilims** (not to be confused with Aryana Tribal Rugs) in Los Angeles. What is more unusual, Mr. Ahmadi has successfully commissioned rugs made in Kabul, Afghanistan. I was surprised when he showed me a good-looking Ushak-like carpet that he produced there. This is the first I have heard of new-era rugs being made in Afghanistan. I can only assume that such production will be sporadic until conditions in Afghanistan improve. But it certainly does suggest some interesting possibilities for the future.

Though Afghan warriors are reputed among the fiercest in the world (they gave the Soviet Union the boot!), most of the Afghan people I know are charming folks who are being pounded daily by civil war, or forced to lead lives as immigrants and refugees. We wish them well and hope for an end to the rancor that divides them.

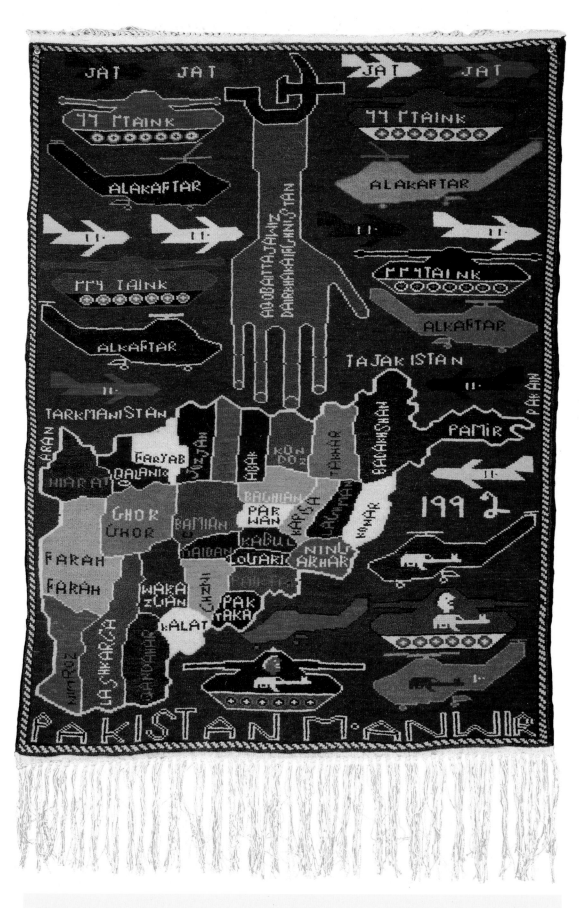

A hand with hammer and sickle attached reaches down from the North to strangle Afghanistan. At the top of the rug we see 'jat' airplanes and 'tainks'. We see aircraft called 'alakaptars'. This is a War Rug, woven by an Afghan refugee (M. Anwar) in Pakistan, 1992. From the collection of Dr. John Sommer. (David Holbrook Young.)

In this War Rug, the hand of the Soviet Union again reaches into Afghanistan, but this time to grasp a figure who himself bears a hammer and sickle. In contrast to the scenes of fighting in the upper half of the rug, we find pastoral scenes below. A battle rages among collectors, too: Are War Rugs works of art, or mere curiosities? Whatever else they are, they are poignant documents of the wars that have ravaged Afghanistan since 1979. From the collection of Dr. John Sommer. (David Holbrook Young.)

This unusual war rug is flat-woven. In it, traditional rug design (the vase and flowers in the center) is mixed with modern machines of warfare (helicopters and automatic rifles) and archaic fighters (swordsmen on horses). A lion battles a dragon. While many variations of the other three war rugs are to be found, this piece seems unique. Could it be a truly personal statement? From the collection of Pat Markovich. (David Holbrook Young.)

Maimana kilim from northern Afghanistan. Maimanas are in good supply now and are very inexpensive. If you look through enough Maimanas, you are sure to find a very worthy piece for little money. The rug pictured is about 3½' by 6', though Maimana kilims are woven in nearly all sizes.

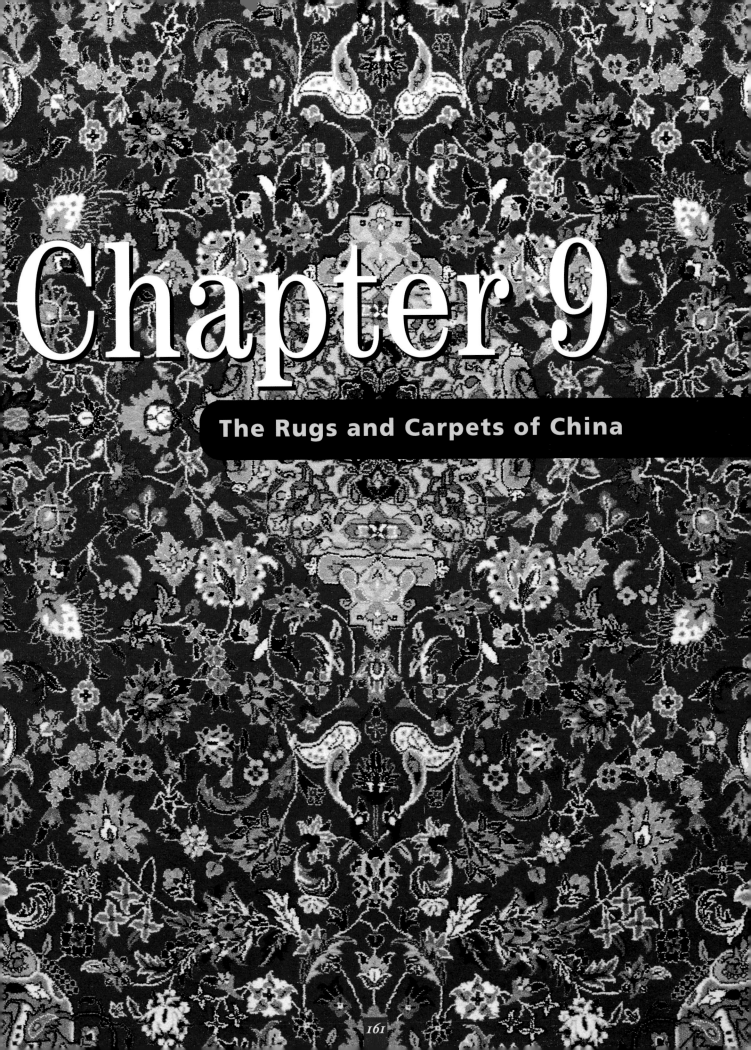

Chapter 9

The Rugs and Carpets of China

For many years the U.S. did not trade with China, which was widely known in America during those days as Red China, a name that suggests why we did not trade with her. At least one respected American rug dealer caught smuggling Chinese rugs into the U.S. was sent to jail by the U.S. government. After President Nixon went to China, the U.S. in 1973 provisionally accorded China most favored nation trade status, and trade resumed.

When trade first opened up to U.S. carpet importers, access to Chinese rugs was by invitation only. A Chinese governmental agency called 'the head office' kept a short list of American Oriental rug firms with whom they were willing to deal. About thirty names were on the list. Peculiarly, the head office encouraged an even smaller group of importers to form a kind of cartel that would have effectively prevented anyone from competing with them. But those who were asked to participate were skeptical about the legality in the United States of such an arrangement, and it did not get off the ground. Foreign buyers conducted business with state corporations and had no direct contact with the manufactories. Buyers selected ready-made stock from government warehouses and had little or no input into what the Chinese produced.

Strangely, the Chinese government did not seem especially concerned about making a profit. Instead, their interest was in keeping people employed. With that as their goal, they had frequent problems with over-production, and at times they were very motivated sellers. Some American firms are said to have walked away from millions of dollars they owed Chinese state corporations with no consequence to themselves. Government losses did eventually cause the head office system to break down. As branches of the head office lost money, they lost clout, and soon they no longer controlled which foreigners were allowed to do business there.

By about 1990, much had changed in the way business was done in China. Essentially anyone with enough money could buy rugs in China. Secondly, buyers began to have direct access to manufactories: they now had input into what was produced. They could discuss designs and color, and, for the first time, China became responsive to the needs of the American consumer. I judge this to be one of the elements that furthered the Oriental rug renaissance. Not very many years later, visionary Americans were commissioning the Chinese to produce some of the best rugs made in the past seventy years.

The very first rugs to come out of China when trade resumed were a handful of mat-sized antique Chinese pieces that, for old rugs, were quite inexpensive. It was said that China misprized native artifacts since they represented her imperial past. The vast majority of the carpets imported from China were the pieces known as **70-line, 90-line and 120-line Chinese rugs**. These were made in traditional Peking designs and colors, with thick pile and excellent wool. The rugs were distinctive in having sculpted pile. The dyes were chrome and their pile was machine-spun. Designs were spare and usually consisted of traditional Chinese motifs. They were an exotic addition to the market when they first appeared and were very popular. But in the 1980s, these classic Chinese rugs became the object of price wars among rug dealers, leading to a situation where no one could make a profit on them. Classic Chinese rugs were banished from many dealers' showrooms by the end of the decade. In the 1990s they had found a niche in some of the large consumer outlets where they are still sold at very low prices, usually in the bottom-end 70-line grade. The design of these and all other Oriental rugs should be visible on their backs. Do not confuse them with rugs made in China, often also sold at consumer outlet stores, that look much the same but whose backs are covered with cloth. These rugs are not knotted: a machine is used to insert pile into their foundations, and they are not Oriental rugs at all. They are even less expensive than 70-line Chinese rugs, but will not last as long and have no individual character.

I was told this story: 'There was a British gentleman who owned a suit that he loved dearly. He heard that Chinese tailors were able to copy anything, so, at his first opportunity, he gave it to a Chinese tailor, asking that he make three suits just like it. He was annoyed, though, when a short time later the tailor produced the three new suits.

A Chinese 'Persian' from Henry Gertmenian Company in San Francisco. It is made with chrome dyes and mill-spun wool. As is typical of these carpets, it is finely knotted, has good wool, is of excellent workmanship and, of course, is based on Persian designs. (David Holbrook Young.)

Except for one thing they were perfect. All three were missing the same button.' This story may say something about some Chinese rugs. Critics fault them for being too-perfect copies. They are without flaw or irregularity. Their edges and ends are perfectly straight, their colors perfectly consistent. A design figure in one quadrant of the rugs is repeated without fail in the other three. The other side of the coin, though, is that their quality control may be unsurpassed.

Paul Gertmenian of the **Henry Gertmenian Company** in San Francisco was one of the first American rug importers on the scene after trade resumed with China. He attended the second China Rug Fair in 1977, and has imported rugs from China since then. When Paul Gertmenian's father, Henry Gertmenian, turned 72, Paul left the ministry to join his father's business. Some other American firms importing rugs from China are much larger, but the Henry Gertmenian Company's inventory of Chinese rugs represents mainstream Chinese production perfectly. The company, for instance, offers an excellent selection of **Chinese Persian rugs**—the ones that, in a sense, have replaced classic Chinese rugs. A name like 'Chinese Persian', which is analogous to calling an automobile a Ford Chevy, reflects the confusing merger of styles, countries, and peoples encountered in today's market. As the hybrid name suggests, they are Chinese rugs made in Persian designs, with elaborate, curvilinear lines. These rugs, with wool pile on cotton foundations, almost always have traditional Persian colors with clear reds. Their wool pile is machine-spun, dyes are chrome. Quality control is excellent, and prices are always very competitive.

China has a unique system of quantifying the fineness of a rug's weave. It is expressed in terms of the number of warp threads strung on a loom in one running foot. For instance, a 120-line rug will have 120 pairs of warps lying side by side on the loom in one running foot. To convert this figure to knots per square inch—the standard way of expressing fineness of weave in the U.S.—divide 120 by 12 (inches) and you have 10

pairs of warp threads in one inch, on which 10 knots will be tied. Chinese rugs have a 'square knot count', meaning that, if ten knots are tied vertically in one inch, ten will also be tied horizontally. So, in our example of a 120-line rug, the knots in one inch are 10 times 10, or 100 knots per square inch. If you are like me, you will forget that formula at least fifty times.

When **Teddy Sumner** of **Michaelian and Kohlberg** took control of his family's business as a young man in 1982, he was too naive to be intimidated by the prospect of manufacturing Oriental rugs. After watching European-style needlepoint carpets, which his grandfather Frank Michaelian had produced in China beginning in 1917, sell at auction for giant prices, Teddy Sumner began a new production of needlepoint rugs in China. The rugs began to come onto the market at about the same time that, by my reckoning, our present rug renaissance began to assert itself, 1985. Many of the prototypes his grandfather had developed were still in storage in China forty-five years after they had stopped being made. Mr. Sumner cleaned them and picked up where his grandfather had left off in 1937. They are in French, Italian, and English styles, very formal and elaborate. Michaelian and Kohlberg produced them uncontested in the marketplace until 1990, and produces them to this day.

In 1990, Teddy Sumner and **George Jevremovic** of Woven Legends cast lots together in a new business called **Black Mountain Looms**. While George Jevremovic concentrated on a joint production in Turkey, Teddy Sumner began to gear up in China for a production of natural-dyed, hand-spun rugs and carpets that became known as **Little River**. Natural dyeing, at least on a commercial scale, was unknown in China at the time, so Black Mountain Looms shipped vegetal dyes from Turkey to China where Mr. Sumner and Mr. Jevremovic set up a workshop and taught Chinese dyers to use them. To teach the Chinese how to spin wool by hand, Black Mountain Looms brought an experienced spinner from Boulder, Colorado who spent ten days training Chinese craftspeople in the technique.

A Chinese needlepoint from Michaelian and Kohlberg in New York. It is called Louis XIV Screen and is made in only one size, 3′ by 7′. Obviously this needlepoint rug is based on exquisite old European designs. Though needlepoint rugs lack body, Michalean and Kohlberg find that they live surprisingly long on the floor.

A Chinese needlepoint from Michaelian and Kohlberg, called Verdure, 3′ by 12′.

A Little River carpet from Black Mountain Looms. There is no other production of carpets in the world I admire more than Little River. They are finely knotted, made with handspun wool and vegetal dyes, finished with no harsh chemicals, and made from the best nineteenth-century designs. This carpet is about 9' by 12' and seems based on an old Ferahan Sarouk.

A Little River carpet from Black Mountain Looms, made in China. Many rugmakers have to bleach colors into submission in order to soften them for a decorative look. Black Mountain Looms simply made good color choices to begin with. It is soft-colored without being washed out.

A Little River carpet from Black Mountain Looms. I have collected a Little River piece like this and count it among my favorite rugs, old or new.

Chinese silk rug. Chinese silks are the real bargains in the specialized silk-rug market. This piece was imported by the Henry Gertmenian Company of San Francisco. (David Holbrook Young.)

In discussing Chinese spinners and weavers, Mr. Sumner mentioned the stereotype about Chinese craftspeople suggested by the story about the three suits—the stereotype, of course, being that Chinese craftspeople are capable but unimaginative. Teddy Sumner disagrees. He believes instead that they are cooperative and happy to please and, he adds, are extraordinarily skilled and flexible. For instance, weavers working for Black Mountain Looms are able to tie both the Persian and Turkish knots. I have never heard before of weavers able to do that.

Today, Little River pieces may be the best carpets made anywhere in the world. Messieurs Sumner and Jevremovic have undertaken to recreate some of the most desirable carpets ever: late nineteenth-century Ferahan Sarouks, antique Bijars, old Tabriz carpets, antique Serapis and Bakshaish rugs, and many more. They have done an intelligent job of simplifying ornate designs, where needed, and made many other good decisions. The finished product is clipped low but is neither distressed nor washed with anything caustic. The weave of about 130 knots per square inch is fine enough for detail and clarity. Naturally, some are more successful than others—especially among the rugs made with vegetal dyes, which are hard to control. But if I had to pick just one kind of new rug to collect, it might be Little River pieces from Black Mountain Looms. Compared to other top-of-the-line rugs, they seem like bargains to me at about $70 per square foot.

Chinese silk rugs are among the most lavish Oriental rugs in the market. I have counted 2500 knots in one square inch of a silk Chinese rug! (Counting them may not have taken as long as you might imagine. To measure knots per square inch, we count knots in an inch running horizontally and in an inch running lengthwise and multiply them. Of course.) Reliable people have told me that one very small silk rug in China contains 7000 knots per square inch and is priced at some ungodly sum like $100,000. Rugs

as fine as the finest silk Chinese rugs allow for the most astonishing shading and detail. I don't believe that anyone can fail to be impressed by them. But not all are as fine as 2500 knots per square inch. Chinese silks are made in a number of knot-counts, starting at about 250. Only Hereke silks from Turkey can compare with the finest Chinese silk rugs in this respect, and Herekes cost far more.

> An American rugmaker I spoke with, personally watched a Turkish dealer buy $500,000 of fine silk Chinese rugs. It was clear to him that they would be sent to Turkey and sold as silk Herekes. Others have reported to me that they have seen fine wool and silk rugs in Persian designs—Nains in particular-made in China expressly to be sold in Iran as Persian rugs. This says much about the quality of Chinese rugs and their relatively low prices. It is also a warning to be on your guard.

Megerian Brothers Oriental Rugs from New York City make among the best European-style carpets, kilims, and tapestries. These most formal looking of all rugs are lavish in design and are exquisitely made.

In about 1995, we began to see **inexpensive kilims from China**, woven in Caucasian and south Persian designs. They were amazingly cheap, but looked it. Every year they have improved, and now they are both inexpensive and very good. We have illustrated a kilim made by Nourison Oriental Rugs of New York. It retails for less than $15 per square foot!

Lately I have seen a small number of Chinese-made carpets woven with Turkish knots. I had thought that all Chinese rugs were made with either the Persian, Tibetan, or Mongolian knot, so I was surprised. But I was astonished to find that each knot has four tufts of wool forming the pile instead of the usual two. I had never seen this before. Apparently weavers double the yarn before they tie it to the foundation, presumably to get a very dense

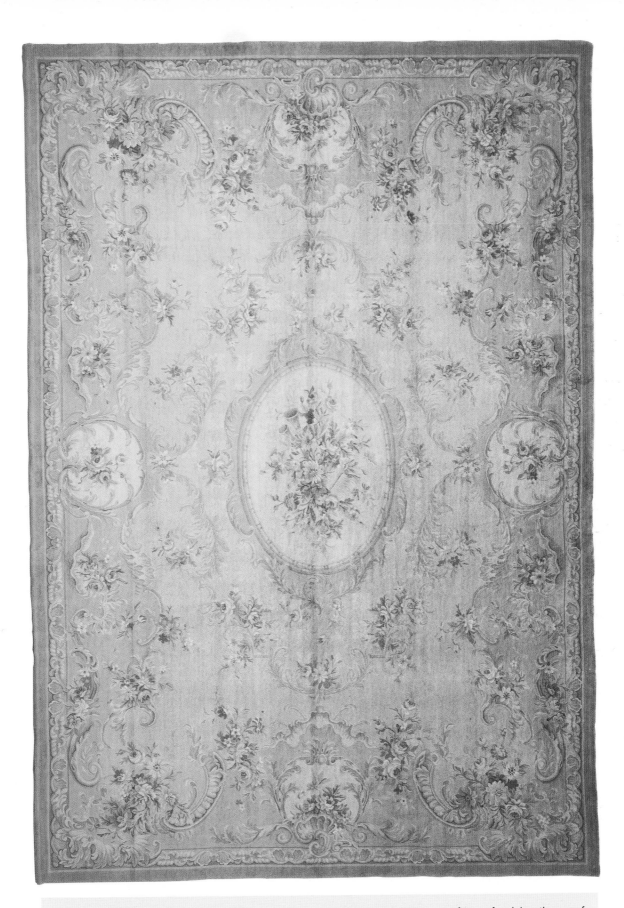

A carpet from Megerian Brothers in a French Savonnerie style. Savonneries and Aubussons are often confused since they are of similar style. Savonneries, though, including this piece, are knotted carpets, while Aubussons are flat-woven. Woven in China. (You may read more about Megerian Brothers in the section about Egyptian rugs, and you will find plates of other Megerian Carpets in the section on the rugs of Romania.).

A Megerian Brothers 'Aubusson'. What could be more beautiful and lavish in design than this sumptuous flat-woven carpet? But are such carpets really 'Oriental rugs'? It is very French. Like many other of today's Oriental carpets, it has surprisingly international origins: made by an Armenian family from New York from a French prototype by Chinese weavers! About 10' by 14'.

surface with a minimum number of knots. I was puzzled by their exact provenance for a day or two, but, by luck, I met **Wenjun Cheng**. Mr. Cheng was visiting from China where he is an agent or broker in the carpet industry. He was originally assigned the job by the Chinese government, but as the structure of the Chinese economy changed, he was allowed to go into business for himself. As an agent, his business is to represent American and European importers. He matches their needs with appropriate producers and makes sure that the quality of the carpets is up to specifications. Mr. Cheng was as surprised as I was to see the four-tufted knots, but he was familiar with Chinese rugs with Turkish knots. He believes that they were made in the town of Hetian in Sinkiang Province, in the far west of China. With the possible exception of Hetian, Wenjun Cheng knows of no center in China capable of producing carpets in a full range of vegetal dyes. He thinks that one or two natural dyes may be used here and there in China, but evidently there is no widespread use. Hand spinning, however, is 'no problem'.

This kilim, made in China by Nourison of New Jersey, is an amazingly effective rug for very little money. It is about 6' by 9'.

Chapter 10

The Rugs and Carpets Of Iran, Egypt, Romania

Gabbeh. The charm of these rugs is their wonderful, shaggy wool pile, the lavish vegetal dyes that are packed into them, and their fetching simplicity. It is sometimes difficult to distinguish Persian gabbehs from the gabbehs made in Turkey and elsewhere. From Ararat Imports, Portland, Oregon.

How strange it seems to include Persian rugs in a chapter on miscellaneous rug-producing countries! Iran dominated the world of Oriental rugs for most of the past century. She produced the most respected city rugs and carpets, as well as a huge variety of good tribal and village rugs. But that is all academic for Americans, now that the United States government has declared Iranian rugs contraband. After Iran's Islamic revolution and the hostage crisis, the U.S. placed a ban on the importation of all Persian goods. Somehow oil was exempted, leaving, for all practical purposes, only Persian carpets on the list. European countries still import them.

It has been very difficult to gather solid information about what is being made in Iran today. A few Persian rugs reach the American market, it is true. Iranians who immigrate to America are allowed to bring a limited number with them as household goods, and some of these make their way onto the U.S. market. Others are smuggled in from Canada (where there is no ban on Iranian imports). Whenever I see them, I am surprised that they are so little changed from a decade ago.

Although Iran seems to have lagged behind much of the rest of the rug-weaving world in the use of natural dyes, there are important exceptions. Tribal weaving is alive and well in the South, at least among the Qashgayi, who are making **Gabbehs** in handspun wool and wonderful, saturated natural dyes. Most are in abstract designs that seem mere excuses to load dye into wool and load wool into a rug. The quality of the wool is unmatched except possibly in Tibet. Most are of moderate knot count, but some, especially those depicting scenes from the countryside, are impressively fine. There is a playful exuberance about these pieces that is charming. They will be very collectible if they ever become available in quantity in the U.S. as they are in Europe.

I see other pieces here and in Europe that, while not natural-dyed, are worthy rugs. Among the standouts are **Yalamehs** (accent the first syllable) which are made in southern Iran, and Bijars (bee JAR) which have synthetic dyes now, but are nonetheless wonderful rugs and still the heaviest-bodied rugs made anywhere. I've also seen new **Baktiaris** that are quite pretty.

America's boycott of Persian rugs must be seriously damaging Iran's carpet industry, but, though down, Persian rugmakers are not out. They have a most amazing history of bouncing back after every catastrophe: the Afghan invasion of Iran in 1722, World War I, the Great Depression, and World War II, among others. Weaving rugs is so deeply ingrained in the culture that it will not soon be lost.

Yalameh. These nice rugs were plentiful in the market before the embargo on Iranian rugs. Now one sees the occasional piece. There are no obvious synthetic dyes in this rug, but because it is rather recent, I assume the dyes are synthetic. It is on a wool foundation and is about 3½' by 5'. (David Holbrook Young.)

Bijar. Bijars are usually thought of as the heaviest-bodied rugs in the entire Oriental rug market. Though this Bijar's colors are pleasant, I believe they are synthetic. I know of no natural gray such as that found near the center of the medallion, and the gold color in the corners lacks the variegation I would expect in a natural dye. It is about 3½' by 5'. (David Holbrook Young.)

Baktiari. One sees a few nice new Baktiaris in the market, and this is one of the most pleasant. Its compartmentalized layout is known as a garden design. A very close look reveals what may be a natural-dyed green. The rug is about 3½' by 5'. (David Holbrook Young.)

Egypt

A young Egyptian man weaves at an A. Moustafa loom near Cairo, Egypt. (Courtesy of Keith DeMare.)

Egyptian rugs are a kind of anomaly, or so it seems to me. On one hand, just a relative handful of rugs and carpets from Egypt reach these shores each year, yet some of these are among the best in the world. Most people don't think of Egypt as a source of Oriental rugs. New Egyptian rugs are almost never included in books on the subject because, first of all, new Oriental rugs of any nationality are rarely written about in books, and, secondly, Egyptian rugs today do not have a recognizable Egyptian 'look'. Nearly all are based on Persian designs.

Egypt has a rug-weaving tradition that dates back to at least the sixteenth century, although, after a brief period of glory, it seems to have gone into abeyance until after World War Two. The birth of the handmade carpet industry in modern Egypt dates to the Egyptian Revolution in 1952, after which the importation of carpets from Iran ceased.

As I was researching the current production of rugs in Egypt, I became aware that a very large Egyptian producer of rugs was just then planning to launch a new U.S.

division. The Egyptian company is **A. Moustafa**, and the president of its American branch is **Keith DeMare**. The Moustafa Company was one of the earliest rug producers in modern Egypt, starting operations right after 1952. Today, Moustafa employs thousands of weavers, young men and women who have reached 15 years of age and have completed nine years of schooling. For some, weaving is a family enterprise, but most are trained by the Moustafa staff.

Moustafa produces rugs and carpets in Persian designs with either Egyptian or Merino wool, or silk, in synthetic dyes and machine-spun pile. The Moustafa family denies that there are more than 'six looms in Egypt' weaving rugs with natural dyes. As this book goes to press, professional photographs are not available of the carpets the company will import to America, but we see glimpses in the photographs of fascinating pieces on the loom or in the process of being finished. It will be interesting to see how a well-established Egyptian firm will fare in America as they jump into the decorative rug market under Mr. DeMare's

An Egyptian Sultanabad from Megerian Brothers. Megerian Brothers carpets are famous for attention to detail and quality control. A combination of natural and chrome dyes are used.

An ivory field Megerian Brothers carpet from Egypt. It too is based on old Sultanabad carpets which, in turn, borrowed from the Persian-rug tradition dating to the sixteenth century and probably earlier.

An exquisite Egyptian carpet by Megerian Brothers Oriental Rugs. Most Megerian carpets from Egypt, like this one, are made after old Sultanabad designs. One of the good things about rugmaking at present is the availability of carpets with green fields. Until quite recently, green was often used as a subsidiary color but rarely found as the dominant field color.

direction. Mr. DeMare's goal? To provide a product as good as the best Egyptian carpets, he says, at half the price.

The most respected American firm weaving rugs today in Egypt is **Megerian Brothers Oriental Rugs** of New York. Indeed, Megerian is among the most respected of all rug-makers today. The Megerian family has been in various facets of the rug business since 1917, including the repair of antique rugs and carpets. Their orientation toward antique carpets and their perception that old carpets were becoming fatally scarce eventually led them to reproduce antique pieces. Brothers **Harry** and **Thomas Megerian** quietly began to make carpets in Egypt, beginning in about 1983, based on old northern Iranian carpets called Serapis. Their sister, **Yeran Megerian**, general manager of Megerian Brothers Oriental Rugs, told me about the early days of the company's Egyptian production. For virtually eight or nine years, the family made one carpet at a time, storing them in the 'basement' until they had collected about 50 pieces. They finally offered them to retailers in the early '90s.

Today, Megerian's Egyptian production is almost exclusively in Sultanabad designs; that is, curvilinear, formal designs based on rugs made in the Sultanabad district of Iran around the year 1900. They are produced with a mixture of natural and chrome dyes and with handspun wool. People outside the family who are familiar with the production attest to the attention to detail lavished on every Megerian carpet. Each is inscribed in Armenian with the Megerian family name; every design is copyrighted. They are among the most expensive in the new rug market, retailing for roughly $125 per square foot.

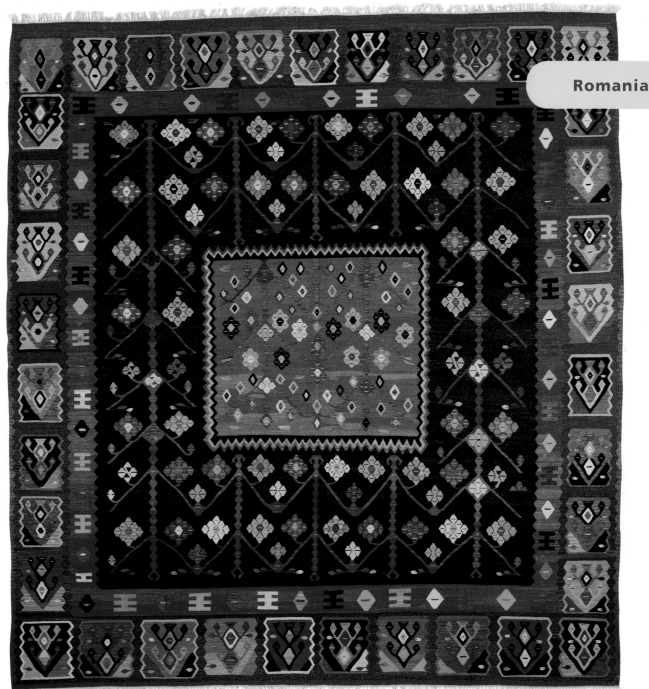

This nice kilim from Black Mountain Looms seems to have been inspired by kilims from Eastern Europe, possibly Romania, where it was made. All dyes are natural.

From the fifteenth century until well into the nineteenth, Romania in Eastern Europe was part of the Ottoman Empire. Even when the Empire dissolved, a Turkish population continued to live throughout the Balkans. There is evidence that kilims have been made in Romania for centuries, and it seems likely that the Turkish population was largely responsible. But Romanian kilims have unmistakable European influences, and it is impossible now to sort out who wove what. In any case, a strong weaving tradition exists in Romania today.

During the late '70s and the '80s, when Romania was still part of the Soviet bloc, knotted carpets from Romania were important in the American market. They featured a shade of rust just as that color was enjoying great favor here. But when the Ceaucescu government was

Obviously modeled after French flat-woven rugs, this kilim from Black Mountain Looms is simple and uncluttered in comparison with other companies' rendering of the same type of carpet. Natural dyes, handspun wool.

Though I could easily find out what this kilim was based on, it amuses me not to. Is it an original work of modern art? A pre-Columbian textile? Sometimes the most ancient designs (such as some of the old Tibetan designs chosen by Stephanie Odegard) strike us as the most modern-looking. This piece was made by Black Mountain Looms in Romania.

overthrown in 1989, the price of labor rose, and many Western rugmakers moved their productions to China and India. Just then, **Black Mountain Looms** arrived on the scene. **Teddy Sumner** and **George Jevremovic**, whose names, for good reason, appear in these pages more than any others, had formed a partnership and were making rugs in China, India—and now Romania (and, on their own, in Nepal and Turkey). In Romania they made kilims especially, but also knotted-carpets known as **Kentwillys** (other Kentwillys were made in Turkey), all in vegetally-dyed yarns brought in from Turkey. Black Mountain Looms' kilims are an eclectic mixture of designs from Turkey, Eastern Europe, and even South America. They are colorful and exciting, finely woven and glowing with health. Kilims in general tend to be unavailable in large, wide sizes. The kilims of Black Mountain Looms are an exception; I have seen them as large as 10 by 14 feet.

Today, Black Mountain Looms is making fewer kilims and hence fewer rugs in Romania. Trucking dyed wool from Turkey to Romania has proved a headache. Trucks break down, border officials demand *baksheesh*. Black Mountain Looms production in Romania is 'on hold'. But there are still plenty of good Black Mountain Looms kilims for sale in the American market.

While Black Mountain Looms is producing less now in Romania, one relatively new company is gathering steam: **Antique Looms** of New York City. Like Black Mountain Looms, Antique Looms is a partnership formed by two experienced rugmakers: **Megerian Brothers** and **Anadol Oriental Rugs**, involving **Harry** and **Thomas Megerian** and **Suat Izmirili**. This unusual alliance of Turk and Armenian seems to have worked well. Mr. Izmirili brings naturally dyed Turkish wool to Romania, where it is woven under Megerian supervision into a very interesting line. **Paul McSweeny**, from Antique Looms, facetiously calls the rugs casually formal—or formally casual. They bridge the gap, he says, between village and fine city rugs. They are made with relatively finely spun wool, on wool foundations in a number of designs such as Mahal, Sultanabad, Karabaugh, Khotan, and Tabriz. The pile is clipped low for an old-rug look, but no foundation shows, and no heavy washing is used to 'antique' them. Antique

Looms is making carpets up to 15 by 30 feet! The company has existed for only about two years, but there is good reason to believe that it will become a major player.

Megerian Brothers Oriental Rugs of New York makes some of the world's most beautiful flat woven rugs and tapestries in Romania. You may read more about the company in the section on rugs of Egypt in this chapter.

Antique Looms made this carpet in Romania. Characteristically, it is somewhere between rectilinear and curvilinear in design, neither tribal nor quite 'city' in feeling. Antique Looms is a rather new partnership formed by Megerian Brothers and Anadol Oriental Rugs. This carpet is 9' by 12'. See page 193 for another Antique Looms rug (detail).

A Tapestry called Boat, made in Romania by Megerian Brothers. 8' 1" by 6' 11".

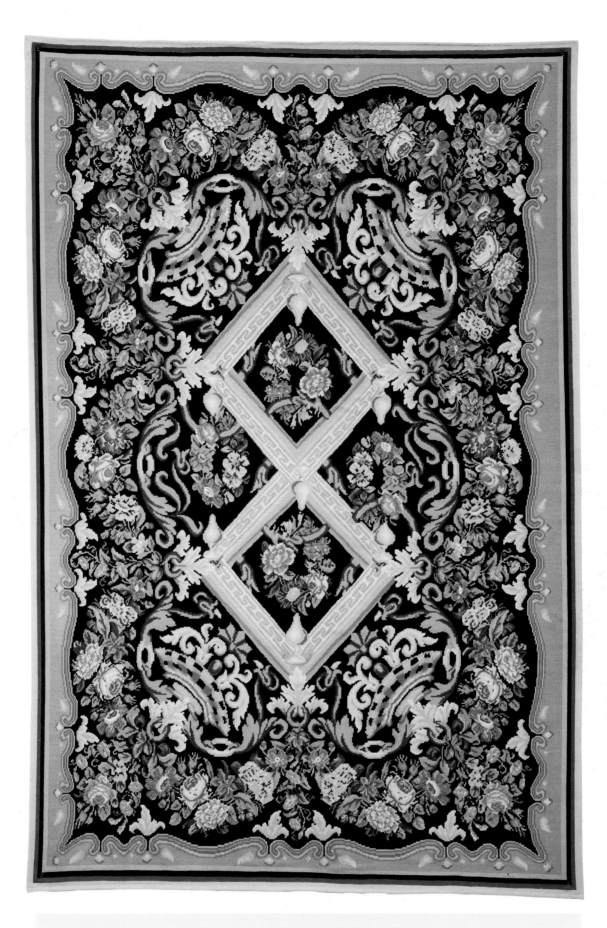

Megerian Brothers made this 'Bessarabian' carpet in Romania. 8' 9" by 13' 1".

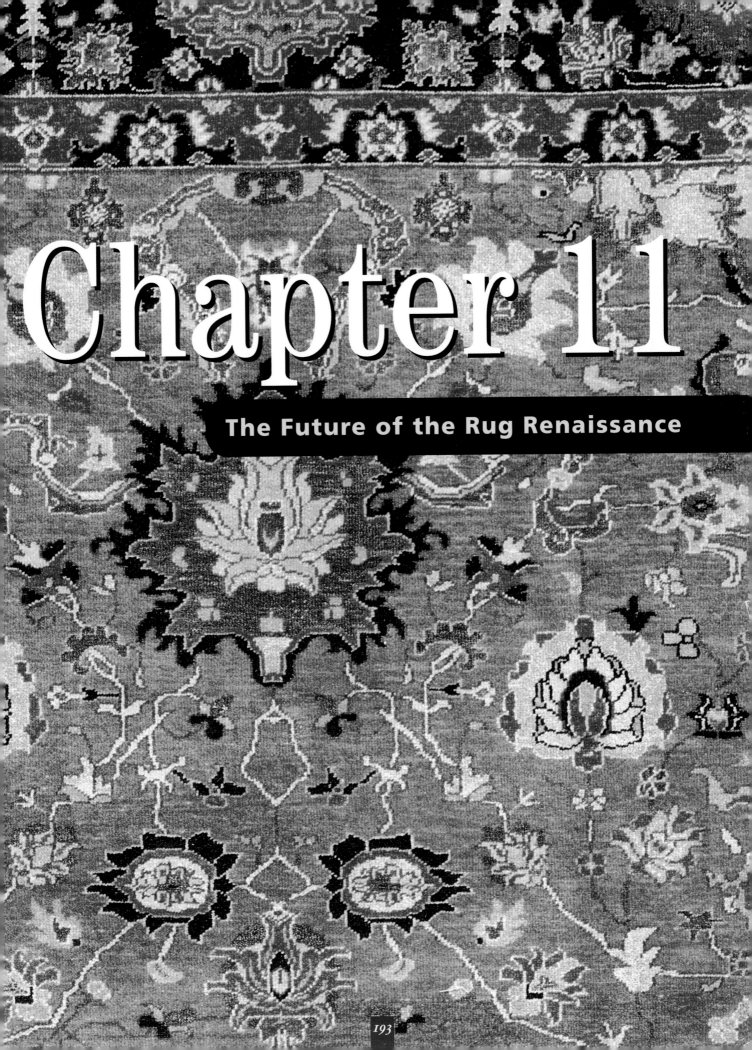

Chapter 11

The Future of the Rug Renaissance

'It is probably fair to say that the best Oriental rugs have already been woven.'
—*Luciano Coen and Louise Duncan*
(The Oriental Rug, *New York and London, 1978.*)

Is it true that the best rugs have already been woven? In the case of Oriental rugs, the past is a hard act to follow. In the Persian Empire of the sixteenth and seventeenth centuries, the limitless wealth of the Safavid dynasty underwrote a golden age of rugs, some may argue, that remains unsurpassed. At about the same time, Mughal India and the Ottoman Empire experienced golden ages of their own, ones unquestionably worthy of the name. It is only prudent to doubt that rugs will ever again be made that match the awesome court products of 400 years ago. Still…

Things change, and anyone trying to predict the future, as do Coen and Duncan above, are likely to go wrong. Nearly thirty years ago, my brother, Murray Eiland, and I used to speculate about the future of rug weaving. Certain things were quite clear to us. Iran and Turkey were industrializing, and weavers there would soon be employed bottling Coca-Cola rather than making rugs. That, as I have said, was thirty years ago, and the weavers are still plugging away. We made other canny guesses too; for instance that Kashmiri rugs were sleepers that would soon be giants in the rug markets. In fact, Kashmiri rugs are still rightly ignored, and Iran is probably less industrialized today than it was thirty years ago. Turkey? Well, we certainly failed to predict that it would be the breeding ground for a rug renaissance, and we completely failed to guess that rugs would enter a golden age in the mid-1980s. Nothing seemed less likely. We did not predict that Richard Nixon would mend fences and trade with China would resume. We didn't dream that the Soviet Union would break up and thousands of Caucasian rugs would pour into the markets from Armenia and Turkestan. We had no idea that Afghanistan would suffer decades of war or that Pakistan would become the effective source of Afghan weaving, nor did we foresee the interminable U.S. boycott of Persian goods. The notion that Pakistan would become the center of natural dyeing or that Turkmen weavers would weave 'Sultanabad' carpets was unthinkable. We did rightly predict that tribal tent and animal trappings would nearly stop being made as nomadism disappeared,

and we were right in thinking that the best old, collectible rugs would become ever scarcer and more expensive. On balance we were miserable prognosticators. Yet here I go again.

Before I make my predictions for the future, let me fantasize about it for a moment. Someday Iran and the U.S. will patch up their differences, and trade between us will normalize. Life in the rug world will become even more interesting. It is impossible to predict what will happen when the mother of all rugmaking countries finally enjoys the stimulus of unrestrained demand from the West. But I believe that Iran will have to use natural dyes again on a large scale to compete in the new market. If it does, the results may be awesome. Imagine Persian weavers across the country once again weaving with madder and indigo-dyed yarns. Iran is one country that perhaps should be left entirely alone to work out the direction weaving will take. But one would hope that Iran, like other weaving nations, would discover their own antique designs rather than carrying on with the inferior designs that they have evolved to. What could possibly be more intriguing than the thought of a 150-year-old Kirman design woven with natural dyes and handspun wool by Kirmani weavers? For that matter, I am ready to place advance orders for Bijars with native dyes. Would Persian Kurds please rediscover their ancient designs, materials, and techniques? And will Hamadan villagers please make again their simple, unpretentious village rugs? If anyone should hear this rug-lover's prayer, please send us Serabs, Serapis, Afshars, Baluchis, Isfahans, Sennehs, Qashgayis, Bijars, and Shahsevans—all in natural dyes, all made by native weavers.

Here is another fantasy. Lately I have seen a few natural-dyed carpets offered at surprisingly low prices—like a 9 by 12 that can be retailed for $2700. I am encouraged. What if natural dyeing were to become so widespread that something approaching mass production of vegetal dyes were to occur and using them were to become cheap? That would not in itself insure that great rugs would be made. But I think it would at least help keep the price of great rugs down. I am especially interested in what would happen if China began widespread use of natural dyes and handspun wool. I rather believe that China may be at the very beginning of its best years of rug manufacture.

Now, let's really fantasize. What happens when Bill Gates falls in love with Oriental rugs? Or, to aim a little lower, what if a government, say that of Turkey or Iran, again finds the spine to underwrite a kind of 'court' manufactory of rugs? That brings us back to the question whose answer so clearly seemed to be yes just a few years ago: Have the best Oriental rugs already been woven? Why no, of course not!

When I first began selling Oriental rugs in 1969, I sold antique rugs exclusively, largely because I loved them, but also because *old rugs were less expensive than new rugs.* I emphasize that because now it seems incredible. Antique rugs were bargains. They could be found in antique stores for practically nothing, especially if they had a hole or two. I regularly sold old 9 by 12 Sarouks for $400 at a time when new Sarouks cost $2500. By around 1975, the tables had turned, and old rugs had become more expensive than new ones. Today we take it for granted that one must pay a premium for antique rugs. But that shows signs of changing again. Sales of old rugs are beginning to suffer, and the prices of all but the best are eroding as new rugs become ever more desirable. At the same time, the best new rugs are growing more and more expensive. It is not at all out of the question that antiques will again become bargains in relation to new rugs. In fact, my first prediction for the future is that within twenty-five years the dialectic will be complete, and thrifty rug buyers will be looking to antique rugs and carpets for bargains.

Consumers will find an ever-greater selection of Oriental Rugs offered on the internet. The problem for online shoppers is that rugs often really are one of a kind, and prices cannot easily be compared. The value of any rug is a much more subjective and personal matter than the value, say, of a book that is exactly like every other copy of the same title. The present wisdom among dealers is that inexpensive rugs sell okay, but that people will not buy expensive carpets on the internet. That may change, though, if rug businesses with an internet presence manage to capture the trust of shoppers over a long time. In any case, consumers can benefit from a large amount of information about rugs available even now online.

The rug industry will be an exciting, turbulent arena. Rug dealers who specialize in antiques will find that their best pieces in excellent condition continue to sell strongly, but that middle and low-end old rugs will not be able to compete with new rugs, and sales will suffer. Eventually there will be even fewer stores than now that sell antique rugs exclusively. Dealers will have to be very well financed to establish inventories of top-end antiques, and will have to be located in the largest metropolitan areas.

Because their customers have been exposed to so much of what is good and currently available, retailers of new rugs will be forced to offer expensive, glamorous rugs with natural dyes, but they will find that they accumulate inventories of unsold carpets passed over by changing fashions. Retailers will have to be inventive, aggressive, and attuned to fashion to stay in business. Some retailers will become manufacturers and a few will succeed.

The genie is out of the bottle. The revolution will not soon go away. Consumers will not settle for boring rugs again. Dealers may come to wish for the bad old days. But I think all this is wonderful. We are in a golden age of Oriental rugs, and long may it continue!

Here are other comprehensive sources for information on Oriental carpets, though you should note that, like most books on the subject, the ones I've cited focus on antiques.

Murray L. Eiland Jr. and Murray Eiland III, Oriental Carpets, *A Comprehensive Guide* (Boston 1998). This book, researched and written by my brother and my nephew, is as close to being the final word on Oriental rugs as it is possible to be at this time. In this edition the work has matured to become not only authoritative, inclusive, and well written, but beautiful as well.

J.C. Ware, *Official Price Guide of Oriental Rugs* (2nd edition 1996). Though its title is misleading—there really is no such thing as an official price guide to Oriental rugs—and though the book's production is not lavish, Joyce Ware communicates in it her deep understanding of Oriental rugs. The book is full of excellent information and quite inexpensive.

Jon Thompson, *Oriental Carpets* (New York 1993). Despite its now politically incorrect cover photograph of young Turkmen girls having a good time weaving (the book was first published in 1983, before today's sensitivity to child labor), this best-selling general guide to Oriental rugs is pure fun. Plenty of good color photos of rugs and rugmakers, tents and nomads, shepherds and stark landscapes make Oriental rugs irresistible.

An online newsgroup for discussion of all matters relating to rugs is at
http://www.orientalrugs.com/public_board/rugpubbd.htm